Escaping the Circle of Hate:

The role of education in building sustainable peace:

by **James Whitehead**

Educational Heretics Press

Published 2003 by Educational Heretics Press
113 Arundel Drive, Bramcote Hills, Nottingham NG9 3FQ

Copyright © 2003 Whitehead, James

British Cataloguing in Publication Data

Whitehead, James
         Escaping the circle of hate:
         the role of education in building sustainable peace
         1.Peace-building 2. International education 3.
         Ethnicity 4. Ethnocentrism 5.Hate
         I.Title
         303.6'9

ISBN   1-900219-26-3

Design and production: Educational Heretics Press

Editorial consultant: Robert Powell

Cover design: John Haxby

Printed by NPM Ltd, Riverside Road, Pride Park, Derby

Preface

The last decade of the second millennium did not deliver the New World Order heralded by George Bush Senior in the immediate euphoria following the collapse of the Soviet Union and the defeat of Saddam Hussein. Despite removing the threat of a nuclear confrontation between the superpowers, in many ways it made the world seem a far more dangerous place. Principally, the emphasis shifted from an environment governed by the fear of war between states, to one where conflict within states is seen as increasingly common and more threatening to international peace.

The causes of such conflicts are understandably diverse, but issues of identity are more often present than not. Specifically, a negative construction of identity, which is competitive and exclusive, asserting the right to uphold your own ethnic, cultural and linguistic identity but not recognising this right for others. If, therefore, we are to avoid or moderate conflict in these cases it appears self-evident that we must transform these negative identities into something more positive. In part, this will require a process of structured learning, in other words: education.

Education, alongside the family, the peer group and, in some cultures, religious observance, is one of the principal agents of socialisation and it is not surprising, therefore, that it should be regarded as a key mechanism for helping resolve conflicts based upon the issue of identity. This may appear to be an obvious conclusion, but it nevertheless gives rise to a whole host of questions, such as: how effective can education be in this context; what needs to be taught and how should it be taught. It is questions such as these that I seek to address in this book.

Acknowledgements

This book is largely a reiteration of a dissertation completed as part of a Master of Science Degree in Global Security at Cranfield University and I am indebted to Professor Chris Bellamy for his guidance and assistance, during both the course and the dissertation. It was truly a life-enhancing experience. I must also express my gratitude to Professor Clive Harber, for his inspirational inaugural lecture to the Chair of International Education at Birmingham University and his guidance on the educational aspects of this dissertation.

I would like to thank Steph and Sheila, the departmental administrative staff, without whom very little at all would get done. They always went out of their way to help and assist me, no matter how stupid the request.

For his assistance in helping me turn my dissertation into a book I am indebted to Robert Powell. Thanks to him the reader will not have to wade through too much academic jargon.

My biggest thank you, however, must go to my wife Avril, whose support, understanding and forbearance over the course of my study was a constant and much needed source of comfort and sanity. Thanks in this regard must also go to my daughter Emily, who was born in the second week of the course and began sleeping through the night only four months later. Without Avril and Emily the dissertation and this book would never have been written.

Table of Contents

List of models, diagrams and pictures

Models:

1.1 Circular Model of Conflict
2.1 Time Dimensions in Peacebuilding
3.1 Theoretical Model
6.1 Transformation Cycle

Diagrams:

3.2 Realist World View
3.3 Liberal World View

Pictures:

5.1 Republician Wall Mural – The Bogside, Derry
5.2 Loyalist Wall Mural – Andersontown Road, Belfast

Introduction

*...since wars begin in the minds of men, it is in the
minds of men that the defences of peace must be
constructed.*

(Preamble to the constitution of the United Nations
Educational, Scientific and Cultural Organisation,
adopted in London 16 November 1945)

i

I trained as a teacher, but decided against secondary education and instead joined the Royal Army Educational Corps, as it was then known, and went to the Royal Military Academy, Sandhurst. Yet despite starting my military career a few months before the collapse of the Berlin Wall and being commissioned eight days after Saddam's invasion of Kuwait, to my knowledge I have only ever been in physical danger on one occasion, and even then it was only very slight. It was in early 1992 and I was riding down the Falls Road in West Belfast with my head, shoulders and arms protruding from the top of a Pig (an armoured land-rover). My head was helmeted, a visor covered my face and in my hands I clutched a rifle. We stopped at traffic lights opposite a line of shops. I was nearest the pavement, and as we waited I scanned the roofs, shop windows and the passing pedestrians. A group of young boys stared belligerently as they went by, telling us bluntly what they felt about our presence. I watched one stoop, reach toward the pavement and pick up a stone; he can only have been ten or eleven. When he straightened up he looked directly at me, pulled back his arm and threw it. Thankfully it flew high. He scowled, his friends laughed, the lights changed and we drove off. Not a piece of high drama I admit, but one that first made me reflect upon the effect that conflict and societal division has upon children. It would be nice to be able to say that this was the point when I first decided to investigate the role that education could play in assuaging conflict, but it was not so. At the time, rather narrow-mindedly, I saw little connection between the two. It was another seven years before the penny finally dropped.

On June 7th 1999, with an end to the war over Kosovo in sight and after ten weeks of NATO bombing, Dr Jonathan Sachs, the Chief Rabbi, spoke on BBC Radio 4's Today programme. His 'Thought for the Day' acknowledged how hard it was to end war, but also emphasised the 'even greater challenge, of sustaining peace'. This, he reflected, would depend upon tackling the 'legacy of bitterness on both sides' and the question he posed was, 'How do you break the 'circle of hate'?' Dr Sachs used the analogy of Moses, who led his people to freedom from Egyptian slavery, and after forty years in the wilderness told his people not to hate the Egyptians. *"If you spend your time trying to destroy your enemies you will end up destroying yourselves."* This same message, Dr Sachs said, must be heeded today by the Serbs and Albanians and will require *"a massive effort of education."* Dr Sachs recognised that, in the short term, *"military campaigns, diplomatic pressure and negotiated settlements"* were necessary, but in the longer term, peace depended upon both *communities* *"learning to coexist, making space for others, letting go of the past and moving on."* He concluded that *"Armies win wars, but it takes education to make peace. Because, though war needs physical courage, peace needs moral courage, the courage to break with the past and turn enemies into friends."* Sachs' words had particular resonance for me, as both a teacher and an army officer, and finally made the link between education and conflict that seven years before had eluded me. They reconciled my two very different professions and offered me an opportunity to contribute from a unique perspective.

At the time of Dr Sachs' broadcast I was part way through a Masters Degree in Education with the Open University and I used the Degree as an opportunity to begin a preliminary search for any connections that already existed between education and the resolution of conflict. Surprisingly, my first tentative steps did not lead me directly to peace education but instead to critical theory, which talked of dialogue facilitated, in part, through education. This led in turn to the work of Adam Curle in conflict resolution. Despite developing a rough theory of how I imagined education might 'break the circle of hate', however, it was not until I began a Masters Degree in Global Security that the links became more obvious. Reading *Man, the State and War*, by the renowned international relations theorist Kenneth Waltz, forced me to think more rigorously about the role of education. In his landmark study into the causes of war written during the 1950s, he took issue with the belief that by changing the nature of man one could reduce the likelihood of conflict. The difficulty was that, while at a theoretical level I had enough material to argue the case for education, I had found little research at a practical level to support Dr Sachs' hypothesis. Help was at hand, however.

Part of the MSc in Global Security included a field trip to Northern Ireland. Not only did I see the Province from a privileged position. It afforded me access to politicians and interested parties of all persuasions and enabled me to ask them if they felt education had a role to play in building sustainable peace in Northern Ireland. Without exception they were adamant that education was crucial to the success of the peace process. In their opinion, a significant factor in the continuance of conflict rested with the behaviour and attitudes of the people of Northern Ireland, and therefore, by altering that behaviour and those attitudes the risk of future conflict could be reduced. By attributing the 'Troubles', at least in part, to a defect in education, it is axiomatic that education can be part of the solution. If this is true in Northern Ireland, it is also likely to be the case in other conflict situations.

There is of course a preferable course of action, which is to prevent conflict from erupting in the first place. This would require instilling in children an antipathy toward violence and bigotry, by establishing positive objectives to guide educational development. In his inaugural lecture for the Chair of International Education at Birmingham University, Clive Harber stressed that the *"twin fundamental goals of education should be peace and democracy"*. This he argued is because *"democracy provides the best environment available for the peaceful solution of disputes and conflicts... While democracies are far from being perfect, accountable and representative government minimizes internal violence and greatly decreases the possibility of going to war without good reason."* The aim of education, therefore, should be to cultivate individuals who:

"Celebrate social and political diversity, work for and practice mutual respect between individuals and groups, regard all people as having equal social and political rights as human beings, respect evidence in forming their own opinions and respect the opinions of others based on evidence, are open to changing one's mind in the light of new evidence and possess a critical and analytical stance toward information. The democratic citizen would possess a proclivity to reason, open-mindedness and fairness and the practice of co-operation, bargaining, compromise and accommodation."

It is obvious that such aims apply equally to post-conflict environments, but what amount of trauma and destruction could be avoided if these values could be inculcated before the threat of violence emerges?

The purpose of this book, therefore, is to consider the role of education in resolving conflict and in building sustainable peace both before and after conflicts. The Introduction has briefly described my motivation for embarking upon this study and why I feel it is important. In Chapter One, I will place education within the context of the broader themes of conflict resolution and establish a framework on which to proceed. In Chapter Two, I will address Kenneth Waltz's criticisms of education in conflict resolution and their salience in the post-Cold War security environment and retrospectively during the Cold War itself. I will then introduce the critical concept of identity, its contribution to conflict, and the work of Manual Castells, whose theory of resistance, legitimising and project identities will be used as a tool in developing a theoretical basis for the role of education in building sustainable peace. Chapter Three will then develop my theoretical framework, which falls out of Castells' theory of identity, and situate my study within international relations and educational theory, the aim being to identify the various theories at work within the field of education and their role or otherwise in building sustainable peace. Chapter Four will consider the practical application of education in a pre-conflict environment, namely Britain, in order to examine the practical role of education in conflict prevention and assess its effectiveness. Chapter Five will then consider the practical application of education in a post-conflict environment – Northern Ireland. The aim, as in the previous chapter, will be to examine examples of education being used in conflict prevention and to assess their effectiveness. The final chapter, Chapter Six, will present a summary of the role that education might play in building sustainable peace and offer a template for future action.

Chapter one

The 'circle of hate'

A world political economy which makes no room for war demands, it must be recognised, a new culture of human relations. As most cultures of which we have knowledge were transfused by the warrior spirit, such a cultural transformation demands a break with the past for which there are no precedents.

John Keegan *A History of Warfare* (1993) pp.59-60

Investigating the link between education and conflict is, I realise, a huge undertaking and one that grew considerably as my research progressed. It should more properly constitute a life's work, rather than a single short book. It is not my intention therefore to produce an exhaustive study of the field of peace education, but instead to explore the role of education in conflict resolution and in building sustainable peace from a number of alternative theoretical perspectives on the basis of two premises:

1. Education is not necessarily always for the good and may actually reinforce the 'circle of hate', referred to by Dr Sachs.
2. A distinction needs to be made between conflict resolution and that of building sustainable peace.

1. The formal system of education, through which most citizens pass, is a powerful socialising force transmitting the values, beliefs, attitudes and behaviours of the dominant group. Education is therefore a tool and its application depends upon those who control it in a particular environment. The depressing reality of this is that education

can be delivered in a moral vacuum and for a variety of purposes, both good and bad. Education is just as capable of producing citizens of a democracy as it is of producing people who will conform, serve the economy, or live according to the prescriptions of a religion.

Totalitarian systems perhaps best illustrate the negative impact of education. The following quote, used by Clive Harber in his inaugural address on assuming the Chair of International Education at Birmingham University, is taken from a letter sent by an American High School Principal to his teachers at the beginning of every academic year:

> "Dear Teacher, I am the survivor of a concentration camp. My eyes saw what no man should witness. Gas chambers built by learned engineers, children poisoned by educated physicians, infants killed by trained nurses, women and babies shot and burned by high school graduates. So I am suspicious of education. My request is, help your children become more human. Your efforts must never produce learned monsters, skilled psychopaths, educated Eichmans [sic]. Reading, writing and arithmetic are important only if they serve to make our children more human."

The Nazis of course also used education to propagate their racial theories at the expense of the Jewish community and other minorities: a practice that continues today. Take for instance the issue of schools in post-conflict Bosnia-Hercegovina:

> "Politicians with difficult problems on their minds rarely think of schools. As the peace was being established it was some time before anyone paid attention to what was happening in schools. When they did look at the education system, they discovered that during the war it had essentially dissolved into three separate systems, each now teaching the next generation a set of political and social values at odds

with the Dayton political agreement and the purposes of the Stabilisation Plan" (Low-Beer 2001).

Education can be a powerful destabilising force within a state if hijacked by extremists. According to P.W. Singer, the weakening of the Pakistani state, as corruption and debt burdens have built up over the last two decades, has led the government-funded education system to the brink of failure (Singer 2001). At present Pakistan spends only 2% of its gross national output on education, one of the lowest rates in the world. The rich elite has responded by sending their children to the increasing number of private schools, but the poor cannot afford this option and the opportunity is seized upon by the Madrassahs (Islamic schools), some of which provide food and clothing, and even pay parents to send their children. The problem is three-fold. In the first place, a radical minority of Madrassahs, perhaps 10-15%, have built extremely close ties with militant Islamic groups and, it is feared, play a critical role in sustaining the international terrorist network. Ironically they were originally allowed to flourish by the government, because they were seen to serve Pakistani interests in Kashmir and Afghanistan. Secondly, by filling a void where the government has failed to provide a basic social service they create a parallel system and diminish loyalty to the state. Finally, the Madrassahs teach a very restricted curriculum, intended for the training of religious scholars and leaders, which makes little contribution to Pakistan's economic prospects. Pakistani President Musharraf has outlined a new policy for Madrassahs, designed to regulate the functioning of these schools and bring their students into the mainstream. It remains to be seen, however, how effective this strategy will be in the face of considerable internal Islamic opposition.

The foregoing account highlights the negative relationship that exists between education and conflict. Paradoxically, however, the fact that education can be utilised to fuel conflict should give us hope that it can also be used to promote peace, although its role in assuaging conflict is palpably less headline-grabbing than the shuttle diplomacy of heads of state and their emissaries, economic sanctions or the use of military force.

2. The difference between conflict resolution and building sustainable peace is that the former represents at best a medium term solution to conflict. In the longer term, if we want to escape the 'circle of hate', we must aim for the larger goal of sustainable peace. My contention, therefore, which is worth repeating, is that 'education' may be used to support the 'circle of hate' and that even a more positive role for education associated with resolving or avoiding conflict will not help in escaping the 'circle of hate' unless it is inspired by the further goal of achieving sustainable peace.

Definitions

Before going any further it is necessary to define, for the purposes of this study, precisely what I mean when I refer to the concepts central to my aim, namely:

1. Education
2. Conflict
3. Sustainable peace

1. There are two important points to be made with regard to education. Firstly, that education is a specific type of learning, and secondly, as has already been discussed, education can be both good and bad. Education and learning are not synonymous. Learning occurs incidentally throughout life. It is the process by which individuals acquire knowledge, skills and attitudes through experience, reflection, study and instruction. Education is an aspect of learning, essentially planned learning. It is artificial and is perhaps best imagined as sitting at the midway point on a continuum between training and indoctrination. Training is about teaching the right way to do something, particularly associated with skill acquisition, while indoctrination teaches the 'right' way to think. In both cases the goals are narrow and there is little or no choice. By contrast,

education has the wider goal of introducing different ways of doing and thinking; it is about the development of choice.

Despite acknowledging the importance of training in the field of conflict resolution and in the preparation of ex-combatants for civilian trades, I will not consider training *per se*. In part, because time and space preclude a thorough investigation, but perhaps more importantly because being geared toward the teaching of specific tasks or skills, training has no direct role to play in the transformation of people's attitudes, although conflict resolution training will undoubtedly have an educational element. This study will also exclude certain categories of education and concentrate upon school age learning, from ages four through to eighteen. This is not to denigrate the value of pre-school education, Further and Higher Education, or Adult Education in the development of sustainable peace. Once again, however, there are two reasons for the exclusion. In the first place the familiar cry of lack of time and space, but also a more important issue, namely, that school is an immensely powerful tool. A child's education, alongside the family and the peer group, is regarded as a key element in early socialisation. The process of socialisation obviously continues throughout life, but these three elements have a profound influence on future development.

2. Conflict cannot be eradicated entirely; disputes, disagreements and arguments are an integral part of what it is to be human. Conflict occupies a wide spectrum, however, from violent to non-violent forms. The aim of conflict resolution, therefore, should be two-fold: to prevent a conflict degenerating into violence and to help reduce those elements of conflict that are inimical to ever achieving a satisfactory resolution or accommodation between different points of view or belief, such as bigotry, xenophobia and intolerance.

3. Sustainable peace suggests a situation akin to the Jewish concept of 'shalom' - an ideal state where armed forces and

weapons are no longer required.   This I fear is a utopian dream; nevertheless, it is a worthy goal and a concept in this study that signifies a break from the 'circle of hate.'

The 'circle of hate'

The central thrust of this book, which is to explore ways of escaping the 'circle of hate', is based upon a circular model of conflict, which was developed by the British Military as one means of conceptualising the future spectrum of conflict and further developed by Christopher Bellamy, Professor of Military Science and Doctrine at Cranfield University (see below).

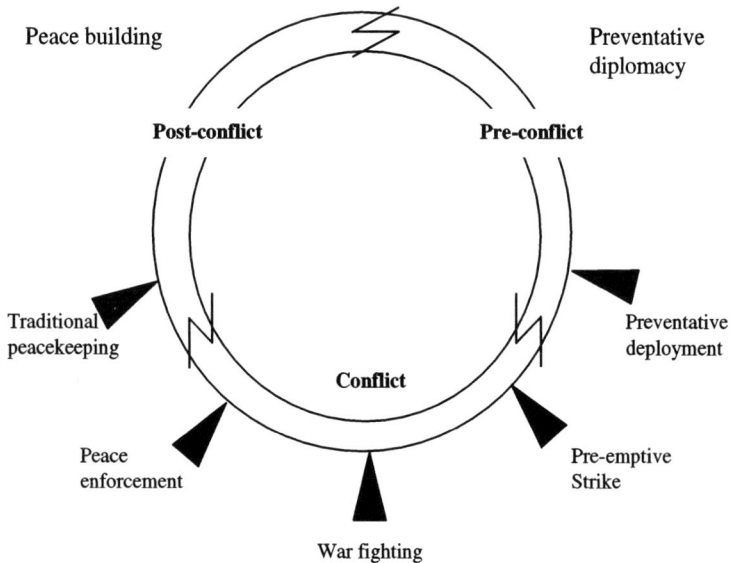

Model 1.1 Circular Model of Conflict.

The model, when viewed from a perspective of searching for peace, easily transforms into the 'circle of hate', referred to by Dr Sachs, a never-ending progression from pre-conflict, to conflict, to post-conflict, back to pre-conflict and so on, with no prospect of escaping this vicious cycle. From a military perspective each stage requires a different approach, ranging from the preventative deployment of troops in the pre-conflict stage, 'traditional' warfighting in the conflict stage, to peace enforcement and peacekeeping as we move into the post-conflict stage. The application of military force alone, however, will not allow us to escape this destructive cycle. Rather than suppressing conflict entirely through force we need to promote peace that is sustainable when the peacekeepers have left. In other words, we need to escape from the 'circle of hate', ideally before conflict has descended into violence, but otherwise when the violence has been contained.

In truth, there is no straightforward solution to escaping this vicious cycle; instead it requires a combination of approaches. These are perhaps best illustrated by General Sir Mike Jackson's analogy of a rope, which has been further developed by Stephanie Blair. The point being that individually the strands of a rope are weak, but when combined together they gain in strength. Taking Jackson's original idea, Blair identified *"four essential strands: the security strand, which creates conditions in which the activities of the other strands can be conducted safely; the political strand, which provides leadership and sets the tone and framework for the others; the economic strand, which provides the incentive for the population to make the transition from war to peace; and the social strand, which supports the transformation of the population."* Education obviously plays its part in the latter strand of Blair's model, helping to transform the attitudes and perceptions of the population in order to avoid a repetition of the destructive patterns that led to conflict in the first place. Considering that education is a primary agent of socialisation, it appears fundamental to this process, sustainable peace will not be achieved without education helping to transform people's attitudes and perceptions.

In the post Cold War world it is increasingly recognised that issues of identity, the psychological ties that bind us into a particular worldview, reinforce these attitudes and perceptions. Manual Castells, in the second volume of a three-volume study of the Information Age, identified three broad categories of building identity. The first, 'resistance identity', is formed by those individuals or communities who reject current forms of authority and seek either to ignore it or replace it with their own authority; the second, 'legitimising identity', is the polar opposite of the first and adopted by those who accept the domination of the current authority; while the third, 'project identity', aims to transform social structures by striving to find an accommodation between these two extremes. In unrelated work on Futures Education, Francis Huthchinson identified the same three categories and described them respectively as 'hopelessness', 'passive hope' and 'active hope'.

It will be apparent that project (active hope) and legitimising (passive hope) identities are essentially alternative routes away from resistance (hopelessness) identities. I therefore use them as a link between the 'circle of hate' and the alternative theories of international relations and education that support them. I am suggesting three such theories, each of which needs to be examined to discover the limitations, if any, they place upon education in this context. The question is not so much whether a theory is 'true', but rather how it constructs the 'truth' and the consequences of accepting it as so. It is from the vantage point of this theoretical foundation that I will then evaluate practical educational experience in a pre-conflict environment (Britain) and a post-conflict environment (Northern Ireland) to identify the practical application of these theories and consequently establish what role education performs. In simple terms do they help to resolve conflict and do they help us break the 'circle of hate'?

Chapter two

A great sea-change

Were half the power that fills the world with terror,
Were half the wealth bestowed on camps and courts,
Given to redeem the human mind from error,
There were no need of arsenals or forts.

Longfellow, H. W. *The Arsenal at Springfield*, 1843

This chapter will make the general case for the role of education in conflict resolution and building sustainable peace. First, I will focus upon the criticisms of Kenneth Waltz, identifying his misgivings about the role of education, but also certain areas of agreement. His criticisms are considered in the broad context of the post-Cold War security environment, dealing specifically with the fundamental problems that he raises. A key issue is the role of identity in fostering conflict, and this chapter will conclude by explaining in more detail the concept of identity and the work of the sociologist Manual Castells, who has identified three broad types of identity building.

The critique of Kenneth Waltz
Kenneth Waltz analysed three 'images' of the causes of war: man, the state and the anarchic international system, but for the purposes of this study I restrict myself to a critique of his 'first image', which locates the important causes of war in the nature and behaviour of man. He argues that proponents of this 'image', which has its roots in the Enlightenment, believe that wars are the result of *"selfishness, misdirected aggressive impulses or stupidity"* and that they therefore conclude that *"if these are the primary causes of war, then the elimination of war must come through uplifting and*

enlightening men or securing their psychic-social re-adjustment" (Waltz 2001, p.16). In the case of the former:

> *"By attributing present difficulties to a defect in knowledge, education becomes the remedy for war."*

And in the case of the latter:

> *"If there were something that men would rather do than fight, they would cease to fight altogether"* (Ibid p.17).

He goes on to say, however, that while one may agree with the first image explanation of war, one need not agree with its subsequent remedies for war. He therefore divides proponents of the 'image' into two philosophical camps: optimists and pessimists. The pessimists believe that reality is flawed and while constraints upon evil can be contrived there is no possibility of a permanently good result. Optimists, on the other hand, believe that reality is intrinsically good, society essentially harmonious and therefore the quality of history can be altered; some would argue for all time. The minimum level of agreement between these two camps, therefore, is that *"the most important causes of political arrangements and acts are found in the nature and behaviour of man"*, but having agreed this fundamental cause the optimists try to change man, while the pessimists give up and turn their attention to political remedies.

Having identified the two schools of thought within the first image, and the pessimists having chosen to search for a solution elsewhere, he turns to the optimists and their remedies for the condition of war. In the first place he re-asserts the distinction (mentioned above) between those who place *"their faith in religious-moral appeals and improved but nevertheless traditional systems of education"* and 'modern' (this was written in the 1950s) behavioural scientists who have undertaken empirical investigations designed to produce a 'prescription for social action'. At which point he makes his view of this latter endeavour abundantly clear:

> *"Relatively few of the total number of psychologists... have turned their hands to the problem of war. Those who have are often those least likely to take a modest view of the contributions of their own discipline. And many articles that are published are occasional pieces written by men who momentarily take their eyes off the white mouse..."* (Ibid p.43).

Waltz argues that psychologists see society as a patient that can be cured either by treating the individuals who compose it or by improving the social arrangements that lead to conflict. The problem he notes, however, is not the understandable plethora of estimated causes and associated remedies, but the *"discouraging vagueness or unrealism both in analysing of causes and in the prescribing of remedies"* (Ibid p.46). For instance, he cites a Professor James Miller, who believed that the cause of peace would be served by planting one thousand trained social scientists in the Soviet Union, disguised as Russians, in order to find out what the Russians were actually thinking. Or another psychologist who believed that delegates to the UN should be required to walk through the playground of a nursery on their way to their meetings. Waltz concludes that *"there is a shortage of systematic attempts to relate the behavioural sciences to the problems of international politics, past, present or future"* (Ibid p.47).

With regard to the optimist school in general he specifically focuses on three major problems faced by advocates of behavioural science and/or education in their efforts to transform behaviour as a remedy for war:

1. The problem of pace
2. The problem of instituting change
3. The problem of dealing with more than one society at a time

1. The problem of pace is concerned with the time required to remodel people and societies for peace, even assuming that it can be determined just what changes are needed – an issue central to my exploration of theory in the next chapter. Coincidentally, Waltz uses the same analogy of Moses in the wilderness, as does Dr Sachs (see the opening paragraph of Chapter 1), but Waltz's interpretation is entirely pessimistic. Moses led his people forty years in the wilderness, because he believed that the re-education of attitudes toward the Egyptians would require the birth of a new generation, which by inference Waltz regards as totally unrealistic and of little practical help in the Cold War environment.

2. The second problem, that of actually instituting change, is two-fold. In the first place it boils down to the simple fact that it appears far easier for society to change education than for education to change society. Taking the example of the Soviet Union, he makes the point that *"one cannot conceive of a change in Soviet education without a prior change in Soviet government"* (Ibid p.56). It appears fruitless, therefore, to press for a change in Soviet education when the object is actually a change in Soviet government, which could be achieved far more effectively by other means. Secondly, he takes issue with the behaviouralists' view that the *"answers to problems exist not in rational solutions, but in the removal of the problems themselves"* (Ibid pp. 56-7). In other words behavioural scientists are interested in getting to the root causes of conflict rather than dealing purely with the symptoms. This he believes is entirely unrealistic.

3. Finally, how does one deal with the added complications that arise when two or more societies must be dealt with at the same time? As an example he takes the work of anthropologist Margaret Mead, who, after a comparative study of cultures, came to the conclusion that ideally we should take the best of other cultures and apply them to our own. For instance, Samoan children do not typically go through the period of adolescent frustration common in the west, because Samoans allow their children to see adult

human bodies and give them wider experience of its functioning. Culture, therefore, not human nature, is the cause of teenage rebellion, and culture can be changed. If western parents, however, were to adopt Samoan practices, in Mead's words they would be building on sand, because once outside the family unit such behaviour would be regarded as unnatural. The root of the problem, of course, is convincing everyone to adopt the new values. Those few perhaps who did would see their children ostracised and in the end cause more harm than good. As Waltz concludes, *"the solution that is rational if substantially everyone follows it may be worse than useless if adopted by a minority"* (Ibid p.54). In the context of international relations the adoption of peace by one state will not necessarily lead to its adoption by others and could in fact lead to a worsening security situation, as the balance of power between the states is altered.

Nevertheless, despite his criticisms of the methods and prescriptions of behavioural scientists Waltz recognises a limited role for behavioural science and education:

> *"If wars are caused by immaturities and anxieties or by the neuroses and maladjustments or by frustrations encountered in the process of socialisation or by some combination of these causes, and if the behavioural scientists can tell us what should be done to remove these causes, we still have a good bit more than half the battle to fight"* (Ibid p.59).

Waltz also makes the observation that *"when idle dreamers awake they either become pessimists ... or they enlarge their analyses to include more of the relevant causal factors"* (Ibid p.76). In the same vein as General Sir Mike Jackson, he recognises that the path to peace requires a mixture of different elements or 'strands in the rope' and concludes that *"the more fully behavioural scientists* [for which I read educators] *take account of politics, the more sensible and the more modest their efforts to contribute to peace become"* (Ibid p.79). There is a degree of convergence therefore, that places education as an element within the overall framework of building peace, but still with a number of fundamental problems to overcome.

The new security environment

The key to challenging Waltz's assumptions is to consider the prevailing international security environment then and now. Waltz was writing in the early years of the Cold War, a period characterised by the threat of nuclear war, superpower competition, the subjugation of Eastern Europe under communism and a marginalised UN. By contrast, the end of the Cold War has seen the resurgence of armed conflict, predominantly within states, and the use of massive violence by terrorist groups. While the risk of major armed conflict between states still exists it has been compounded by the dangers of economic dislocation, crime, drugs, environmental degradation, resource depletion, state collapse and the re-emergence of religious and tribal tension. Many of these tensions, however, are not new. Caroline Kennedy-Pipe argues that:

> *"Limited wars, ethnic conflicts and low level warfare have been perennial features of the twentieth century international landscape, but... the Cold War distorted and narrowed our understanding of the nature of global politics; perceptions of war, conflict and peace became focused upon nuclear war and strategy to such a degree that it was possible to avoid a serious and sustained discussion of issues such as civil war and ethnic conflict"* (Jones & Kennedy-Pipe 2000, p.9).

She goes on to say that although the Great Powers avoided war on European soil, the dynamics of the Cold War provided fertile ground for war in the non-European world. Conventional wars were incorporated into Cold War competition, thereby actually facilitating lower-level clashes in the form of proxy wars. Furthermore, she continues, it should be remembered that this was a period of decolonisation, which engaged many European powers in small wars (Ibid pp.12-13). The failure to think more widely can be attributed to the dominant mode of analysis during the Cold War, which was preoccupied, particularly during the 1980s, with deterrence theory and the northern hemisphere. Little thought was given to the effect of culture and values upon security, religious fundamentalism and the role of sub-state actors in previous eras were ignored and the non-military components of security were neglected. In short, since Waltz wrote his critique, there has been a fundamental change in the security environment and more importantly a change in our perceptions of that environment, which enable us to challenge his conclusions. Additionally, the problems he raised can be countered more specifically.

The problem of pace
Waltz's pessimism over the time-scale needed to achieve the transformation of a society is both accommodated and challenged by the acclaimed conflict resolution theorist John Paul Lederach. In addressing *"the goal of moving a given population from a condition of extreme vulnerability and dependency to one of self sufficiency and well-being"*, Lederach puts forward two key requirements necessary to move us out of the circle of hate once the immediate needs of *"crisis-orientated disaster management"* have been met. The first requirement is *"transformation"*, moving the conflict from confrontation toward negotiation and *"dynamic, peaceful relationships"*. The second requirement is *"sustainability"*, which *"indicates a concern not only to initiate such movement but also to create a proactive process that is capable of regenerating itself over time - a spiral of peace and development instead of a spiral of violence and destruction"* (Lederach 1999, p.75). An approach best illustrated in the model below:

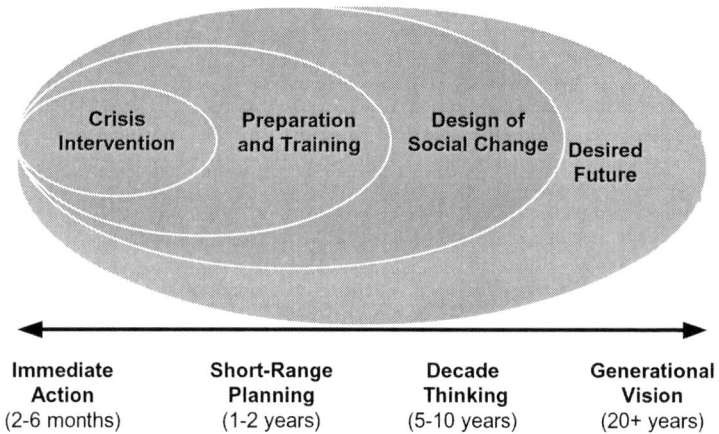

Model 2.1 Time Dimensions in Peacebuilding.

In the model, the first circle represents short-term crisis intervention. This is the period when humanitarian aid agencies would offer emergency relief and those dealing with the conflict itself, such as UN forces, would attempt to halt the violence and achieve a ceasefire. The focus in this stage rarely goes beyond a few months and is aimed at alleviating the immediate suffering and providing the conditions for negotiations to take place. The second circle refers to the realisation by the international community that with the proliferation of humanitarian crises they must better prepare themselves. Training therefore focuses on the 'skills needed to better assess and deal with crises resulting from violent internal conflicts.' The third circle represents attempts to link the immediate experience of crisis to a vision of a better future. The concern here is to put in place mechanisms that will make that transition possible, by creating a sustainable process that will carry us toward that vision. The final circle represents that vision and deals in terms of generations to come, whom, it is hoped, will live in 'more peaceful and harmonious circumstances.' Lederach refers to the work of another key conflict resolution theorist, Elise Boulding, who talked about 'imaging' the future, the necessity within conflict settings to envision a commonly shared future, articulating distant but nonetheless desirable structural, systemic, and relationship goals. The need for a vision is, as Lederach points out *"quite simple: if we do not know where we are going, it is difficult to get there. This time frame provides us a horizon for our journey".* In other words it is the foundation for Castells 'project identities' and Hutchinson's concept of 'active hope'.

While accepting that this is not a 'literal formula' Lederach concludes that *"we cannot respond with quick fixes to situations of protracted conflict. We must think about the healing of people and the rebuilding of the web of their relationships in terms relative to those that it took to create the hatred and violence that has divided them"* (Ibid pp. 76-9). In other words, transformation will take time, perhaps a generation or more, but it is vital if we are to build sustainable peace. Moses' forty year trek through the wilderness is therefore a fitting analogy, but cast in the positive light of Dr Sachs, rather than the more negative terms of Waltz.

The problem of instituting change and of dealing with two societies simultaneously

Waltz, however, would argue that there is no guarantee of a solution even in this longer term, because of the behavioural sciences conviction that they can address the causes of war not just the symptoms. (This is a tension that still exists today between the US administration's 'War on Terror' and its liberal critics.)   In explaining his fundamental disagreement with this view Waltz used the analogy of spectacle wearers, who must resign themselves to wearing spectacles to compensate for their condition and accept that there is no effective remedy for the actual problem.   That was, if the reader will pardon the pun, rather short-sighted and neglected to consider the remarkable capacity of man to overcome seemingly intractable problems, in this case with laser surgery.   Waltz's approach was characteristic of the Cold War security environment, but need not be the case anymore. As George Robertson observed as NATO Secretary General:

"We didn't have to define our security agenda – the Cold War defined it for us.   It was, in a sense a negative agenda: preventing an attack against us.   In other words, security in the Cold War was essentially about things we didn't want to happen... We can afford to be much bolder now.   Rather than thinking about what scenarios we wish to avoid, we can look ahead and design a preferred scenario of the future we actually want."

In the post-Cold War environment attention has shifted to intra-state rather than inter-state conflict, exhibiting the new reality that the majority of states are multicultural and social and cultural causes transcend national boundaries and undercut national allegiances (Kennedy-Pipe op cit p.15). What has emerged is conflict based upon conflicting identities, alongside more traditional struggles for territory or resources, to which the West must respond for reasons of both moral obligation and enlightened self-interest.   The events of 11 September 2001 have only served to reinforce this imperative.   As Rupert Cornwell observed in *The Independent*, the *"attacks did not make the world a more dangerous place. They made the world realise how dangerous it already was"*.

Based upon empirical data available from the Stockholm Peace Research Institute (SIPRI) yearbook in 1989 Kumar Rupesinghe observed that most armed conflicts take place in the developing world and that the basic issues are related to internal matters (Rupesinghe 1992, pp. 52-3).   Ten years later little had changed.   Of the twenty-seven major armed conflicts throughout the world in 1999, which SIPRI defines as more than 1000 deaths in a single year, only two were inter-state (SIPRI Yearbook 2000, p.15).   Waltz's preoccupation with inter-state conflict, particularly that between the superpowers, led him to conclude that to change the education system in the Soviet Union would require a change in the Soviet government and was therefore a futile consideration. In the context of internal conflict, however, it is within the power of the government to use education as a tool in dealing with calls for autonomy and secession; witness the banning of teaching Kurdish in Turkish schools in an attempt to dampen the appeal of Kurdish nationalism. Conversely, in Pakistan, religiously funded schools (Madrassahs), which are accused of breeding Islamic militancy, have filled a vacuum left by the central government's under-investment in state education (Singer 2001).

At least in the case of Pakistan the central government still has the ability, however circumscribed, to influence its education system.   In states fractured by more severe conflict there may be no central government. The situation may have degenerated to such an extent that the state is said to have 'failed', i.e. it can no longer govern its own society and international support is required to ensure order. In this instance it will depend upon the power of external agencies, as to whether an education designed to re-build and transform the shattered state can be provided. Furthermore, with such a power broker(s) in place, the problem of dealing with two societies at once and the danger of instability it might produce can largely be neutralised – not forgetting, however, the notable failure of the UN and the US in Somalia.

Identity conflicts
The SIPRI handbook 2000 stated that in 1999 ethnic identity was a strong defining characteristic in over half of all major armed conflicts. Rupesinghe observed a similar statistic in 1989 and described them as *"the most pervasive and most violent."* He defined identity *"as a sense of self and a sense of the relationship of the self to the world"* (Ibid p.57). In the words of William Bloom, this *"identification is an inherent and unconscious behavioural imperative in all individuals. Individuals actively seek to identify in order to achieve psychological security, and they actively seek to*

maintain, protect and bolster identity in order to maintain and enhance this psychological security, which is sine qua non of personality, stability, and emotional well being" (Bloom 1990). In their study of sectarianism in Northern Ireland, Joseph Liechty and Cecelia Clegg made the important distinction between negative and positive identities. *"At a basic and primitive level"*, they observed, *"a person or group always knows, in part, what it is by what it is not"*. A regrettable consequence of this negative identity is that groups and individuals are often led to avoid certain courses of action, however sensible, because they are identified with the 'other' group. It is this 'mis-shapen logic' that perpetuates and sustains conflict (Liechty and Clegg 2001, p.78). Nevertheless, because the *"needs for belonging, identity and the free expression of difference are basic to humanness"*, they believe that *"a path beyond sectarianism must be one of transforming or redeeming it, not smashing it"*. The power of sectarianism (or the creation of negative identities) lies in the fact that it is a distortion of basic human needs (Ibid p.117).

The recognition that local identities are a source of conflict has much to do with changed perceptions in the post-Cold War period. Notwithstanding the effect that the end of the Cold War undoubtedly had, however, the re-emergence of local identities appears to owe more to the countervailing trend of globalisation - the increasing flow of goods, technology, people and information across international borders. As Cohen and Kennedy observe, confronted by the gathering pace of globalisation, which brings about profound social change and disruption to existing social and political relationships, *"people reach out to the habitual, to the communities where they find familiar faces, voices, sounds, smells, tastes and places... Confused by the effects of post-modernity, relativism and the deconstruction of their known world, they re-affirm and reify what they believe to be true"* (Cohen & Kennedy 2000, p.343).

The danger here, however, is to fall into the trap of many policymakers, which is to believe that the causes of internal conflict are simple and straightforward; namely ancient hatreds that have been re-ignited by the collapse of authoritarian rule in the post-Cold War period, and conclude, therefore, that either the situation is hopeless and must either be militarily contained, or allowed to burn itself out. Yet, as Michael Brown makes clear, the *"single-factor explanation... cannot account for the significant variation in the incidence and intensity of internal and ethnic conflict"*. Instead, he identifies four elements that contribute toward internal conflict: structural factors, such as ethnic geography; political factors, such as exclusionary national ideologies; economic and social factors, such as discriminatory economic systems; and cultural/perceptual factors, such as problematic group histories (Brown 2001 pp.4-5). There are other factors within these four elements, but I have chosen to highlight those which reinforce negative identities to highlight that identity is a dark thread running through all the different causes of conflict and, like the different strands in the rope required to build sustainable peace, the causal factors of conflicts are themselves multi-faceted. The causes must, therefore, be countered by a variety of means, including education. What is beyond doubt is that if we are to move conflicts beyond the 'circle of hate' a transformation from conflict sustaining identities is essential and a useful theoretical tool for this purpose is supplied by the work of Manual Castells.

Manual Castells – three forms of identity building
The sociologist Manual Castells agrees with the belief that the growing recourse to local identities is a reaction against the contradictory trend of globalisation, noting *"the widespread surge of powerful expressions of collective identity that challenge globalisation and cosmopolitanism on behalf of cultural singularity and people's control over their lives and environments"* (Castells 2001, p.2). As well as describing this trend, he hypothesises that generally speaking, whoever constructs collective identity largely

determines its meaning and symbolic content for those identifying with it and those placing themselves outside of it. Consequently, he proposed that *"since the social construction of identity always takes place in a context marked by power relationships"*, a distinction can be made between three forms of identity building: Legitimising, Resistance and Project Identities (Castells pp. 7-8).

- A legitimising identity describes those who accept the current authority and its division of power.
- A resistance identity describes those who reject current forms of authority and power.
- A project identity describes those who wish to transform social structures, through social and political action, hoping to find an accommodation between these two extremes.

Put simply, there is a tension between globalisation and identity, as the complexities of globalisation develop people search for identities that help them make sense of their world. These identities can either be inactive acceptance of the status quo, reactive denial of current authority (i.e. ethnically based nationalism, religious fundamentalism, drugs or crime) or a pro-active desire to change the current reality (i.e. feminism or environmentalism). It is this hypothesis that forms the basis for the development of my theoretical model in the next chapter.

Chapter three

Hope versus history – a theoretical model

To me education is a leading out of what is already there in the pupil's soul. To Miss Mackay it is a putting in of something that is not there, and that is not what I call education, I call it intrusion.

Muriel Spark *The Prime of Miss Jean Brodie*
(Penguin Books, London 1965, p.36)

Having established that education does have a role to play in conflict resolution, we must return to the fact that not all education will lead us out of the circle of hate and some will positively reinforce it. As the reader will no doubt be aware the views of Miss Jean Brodie and Miss Mackay are still central to educational debate. In order to establish which approaches to education contribute toward building sustainable peace and which do not it is necessary to examine each in turn.

Working on the premise that we wish to move away from what Castells describes as 'resistance identities' it is possible to isolate three main theories, see the model below. While not exhaustive of all nuances and similarities each falls neatly out of the three broad categories of international relations theory - realism, liberalism and critical theory – and lead to three distinct practical approaches to peace education. The three alternatives therefore progress from different ways of challenging resistance identities toward distinct approaches to building peace. There are two further streams, however, added at the top and bottom of the model, which respectively represent the extreme expressions of legitimising and project identities. Despite being politically contradictory they share remarkably similar dangers and only offer peace by violent identity suppression and diktat.

3.1 Theoretical model

Response to Resistance	International Relations Theory	Educational Theory	Strategy for Peace
Reinforce	Totalitarianism	Indoctrination	---------
Legitimise	Realism	Traditional	Peacekeeping
Legitimise/Project	Liberalism	Modernist	Peacemaking
Project	Critical Theory	Progressive	Peacebuilding
Revolutionary	Totalitarianism	Indoctrination	---------

The model begins on the left with the possible responses to Castells' concept of 'resistance identities', which he defines as:

> *"Generated by those actors that are in positions/conditions devalued and/or stigmatised by the logic of domination, thus building trenches of resistance and survival on the basis of principles different from, or opposed to, those permeating the institutions of society."* (Castells op cit p.8)

Resistance identities are manifest in forms that are familiar to us all through the media – ethnic nationalism, religious fundamentalism, crime and drug use. They are defensive or escape identities, driven on the one hand by the desire for psychological security: via the familiar and explicable, or through drug-induced oblivion; and on the other by the economic imperative of survival, as economies around the world open up to global competition leading to increasing unemployment and perceived or actual inequality. The response to the growth of resistance identities, in Castells' view, is to support one of two alternative identities: legitimisation, which seeks to rationalise the present system, or a project identity, which aims to transform the existing social structures, through social and political action. It is from these alternatives that the main theories develop and your choice of approach to Peacebuilding, therefore, depends upon your political worldview - realist liberal or radical – as does the educational prescription that emanates from it. Before pursuing these discourses, however, I wish to briefly examine and discard the extreme responses to resistance, which characterise both ends of the spectrum and are inimical to any positive notion of Peacebuilding, only serving to reinforce the 'circle of hate'.

Totalitarianism
The ultimate form of legitimisation is totalitarianism, which can be engineered by political or religious elites using resistance identities for their own ends. In a totalitarian society the political rulers control every aspect of private and social life in the society, as well as having so extensive a political power that virtually no liberty or autonomy in decision-making is left to individuals or groups outside the political power system. Nazi Germany was totalitarian, not because it was a one-party state, where only the Nazi Party wielded power, but because of the way it wielded that power. The whole of the media, the educational system, social, sporting and leisure activities were all controlled by the party and used to propagate the ideology of the Nazis. German society was completely permeated by the personnel and ideas of the ruling group. The Nazi system was built upon a virulent strain of nationalism, but an equally totalitarian system could develop from religious beliefs, where the believers are able to penetrate and organise all aspects of life in a theocratic state, which is what the Taliban attempted to do in Afghanistan.

Iran is the best modern example of a theocracy, but the Iranian Revolution of 1979 also allows us to visualise the emergence of totalitarianism from the other extreme, beyond project identities. In this case the transformation of social structures by social and political action is taken to its utmost, resulting in the violent overthrow of the existing regime. The most instructive illustration of this revolutionary path to social change and the emergence of a totalitarian system is of course the Russian Revolution of October 1917. Through their subsequent use of party appointed officials in all sectors of society, including the military, the Communist Party of the Soviet Union achieved total penetration of the state and the Party's level of control came to epitomise what we mean by totalitarianism. The point is that no matter how noble the goals of revolution the act of abolishing the dominant power is often little more than the replacement of one set of coercive power-bearers for another.

In both cases the education system was a fundamental tool in establishing control, through the use of indoctrination. Quoting from a leading pedagogical manual in the Soviet Union, Hedrick Smith takes the following passage: *"The objective of educational work in socialist society is the formation of the convinced collectivist, a person who does not think of himself outside society"* (Smith 1986, p.200). From his observations, of his 5 year-old son's progress through kindergarten and junior school, he noted efforts, *"however well-meaning, to smother initiative and spontaneity"*. For instance, the children of his son's class produced identical pictures of a flower *"in the same position, with the same number of flowers, in the same colours with the same three leaves on the stem"* (Ibid p.201). The collective conditioning, Smith observed, continued into the school years and in a succession of children's organisations, such as the Octobrists, Young Pioneers, and Komsomol, which are strikingly reminiscent of the Hitler Youth in Nazi Germany.

In a recent study of the Nazi indoctrination of German children, Guido Knopp wrote that, *"alongside the family and school, the Hitler Youth became the third officially recognised bearer of educational responsibility – an instrument of state power with which to imbue the adolescent generation with the spirit of National Socialism"* (Knopp 2002, p.10). In reality, in the opinion of Paul Stuben a former Hitlerjunge (Hitler Youth), *"Parents gave up their right to educate their children when boys joined the Hitler*

Youth" (Ibid). Membership remained voluntary until 1939, but very few children could stand up to the *"all-pervasive pressure ... of belonging to the great community"* (Ibid p.11). The Hitler Youth emerged as the youth wing of the Nazi Party and therefore existed before Hitler became Chancellor.

Once in power, however, Nazi ideology was also introduced to the classroom and school textbooks and guidelines for teachers changed accordingly. Any teacher who refused to accept the new prescriptions had to leave their job. School became a place to instil *"hateful images of the Jews, and the right of the stronger."* In Hitler's view, education was about rearing healthy bodies and developing *"war-worthy qualities of character"*, loyalty, courage, endurance, obedience and willing self-sacrifice (Ibid p.120). The educational system became entirely subordinate to Nazi ideology and helped reinforce the circle of hate. In these circumstances, Communist or Fascist, any sort of 'peace' would be of a type imposed from above by force of conquest, subordination or elimination of undesirables, who objected to the legitimacy of the ruling Party. It would therefore be at the expense of democracy and freedom of choice. I therefore discard these extremes as unsuitable vehicles for the development of sustainable peace and turn instead to the three more moderate approaches.

Legitimising identity - realism and traditional education
The first discourse emerges from Castells' legitimising identity, which is *"introduced by the dominant institutions to extend and rationalise their domination"* (op cit p.8). This approach finds its theoretical expression in the realist account of international relations, which is widely regarded as its most influential theoretical tradition. As the name implies, realism seeks to describe and explain the world of international politics as it is, rather than how we might like it to be. As Scott Burchill makes clear, realists are pessimistic about the international political system, which they see as *"characterised by conflict, suspicion and competition*

between nation-states", and is therefore unlikely to yield to changes in structure. *"For realists"*, Burchill continues, *"international politics is a world of recurrence and repetition, not reform or radical change"* (Burchill 2001, p.70). Crucially, realists distinguish between an international political environment, which is without central authority, and therefore anarchical and hostile, and an ordered, hierarchical domestic environment. The aim of the state is to maximise its interests in this hostile environment, which is based upon three concepts: survival, self-help and statism. A worldview illustrated in the diagram below:

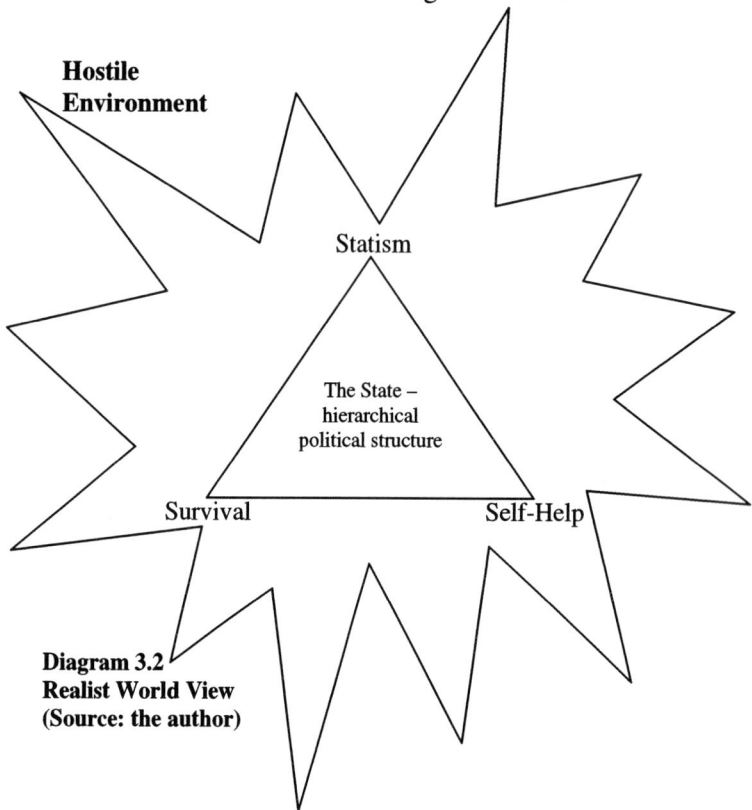

Hostile Environment

Statism

The State –
hierarchical
political structure

Survival   Self-Help

**Diagram 3.2
Realist World View
(Source: the author)**

The core national interest of any state is survival; the pursuit of power and the promotion of national interest is paramount. All other considerations, economic, environmental, humanitarian and so on, are subsidiary. Self-help is the guiding principle of action in this anarchical environment. Realists do not believe that it is prudent for a state to entrust its safety and survival to another actor or international institution. If a state feels threatened, it should augment its power, which is narrowly defined in military-strategic terms, i.e. the ability to get what you want through the threat or use of force. Finally, and most importantly for this study, is the concept of statism: the belief that the state is the legitimate representative of the collective will of the people and is therefore able to impose order within its own boundaries.

Alongside a capacity to deter external aggression, the ability to impose order within its own borders is an equally key requirement for any state. As Clive Harber points out, *"Historically, one of the major reasons for the establishment of modern mass schooling systems was as a form of social and political control"* (Harber 2002, p.8). It was designed, he continues, *"to counter the threat to the state of increasingly industrialised, urbanised and potentially organised working populations"*. Harber cites Andy Green's study of the origins of mass schooling in France, Germany, the UK and the US which argues that *"The task of public schooling was not so much to develop new skills for the industrial sector as to inculcate habits of conformity, discipline and morality that would counter the widespread problems of social disorder"* (Green 1990, p.59). Schooling was organised *"to prepare future workers with the subordinate values and behaviours necessary for the modern bureaucratic, mass production workplace and the existing social order"*. The social control function of modern mass schooling systems has been seen at its most overt and obvious form in the totalitarian systems of Nazi Germany and the Soviet Union. It, however, *"was also gradually extended globally from European societies through colonisation where the purpose of schooling was to help to control indigenous populations for the benefit of the colonial power ... Subsequently, in Africa, many post-colonial governments did not hesitate to use schooling for political control purposes of their own"* (Harber op cit p.9).

Realism, therefore, finds its educational expression in what can most simply be described as 'traditional' education, an outlook that still exists today. In an analysis of the evolution of the 1988 Education Reform Act in the UK, Stephen Ball traced and identified three broad strands of educational theory that had impacted upon its development over the preceding years: Traditional, Modernist and Progressive' (Ball 1990, p.43). Those defined as 'traditionalists' emphasised the role of education in promoting national culture and maintaining academic standards. They had an academic approach to provision and emphasised the cultivation of literary and aesthetic sensibilities, the reproduction of culture and moral subordination. Traditionalists believe in strong state control over educational institutions and curriculum, the proscription of non-subjects (those outside the traditional range of Maths, English, History, Geography etc.) and an apolitical curriculum. The relationships between tutors and learners are formal, and assessment and selection are both summative (exams at the end of term for example). Although a degree of caution is required when extending these broad categories of educational theory to other nations that does not mean that similarities of influence cannot be identified. The above quotation from Harber illustrates how traditional approaches to education spread through colonialism and such diffusion is still present, if not accentuated, given the even greater global integration being experienced in the contemporary world.

Legitimising project identity - liberalism and modernist education

The second discourse, associated with both legitimising and project identities, emerges from the liberal tradition, within which, as Scott Burchill explains, there exist *"two quite distinct and at times contradictory sub-traditions within a broad philosophical outlook"*. On the one hand an ethical view that *"has advocated political freedom, democracy and constitutionally guaranteed rights, and privileged the liberty of the individual and equality before the law",* and on the other a market view, that argues for *"individual competition in civil society and claim[s] that market capitalism best promotes the general welfare by most efficiently allocating scarce resources within society"* (Burchill op cit p.29). Traditionally, in the field of international relations, liberalism has been the natural opponent of realism, because unlike realism it is a tradition of optimism. Whereas realists believe the world to be irrevocably fixed, liberals argue that the international political system is the product of ideas and, crucially, ideas can change. Significantly, however, liberals share with realists a common belief in the primacy of the state within a hostile international environment. Yet in contrast to the realists, liberals offer a co-operative rather than an antagonistic remedy for state survival, as below:

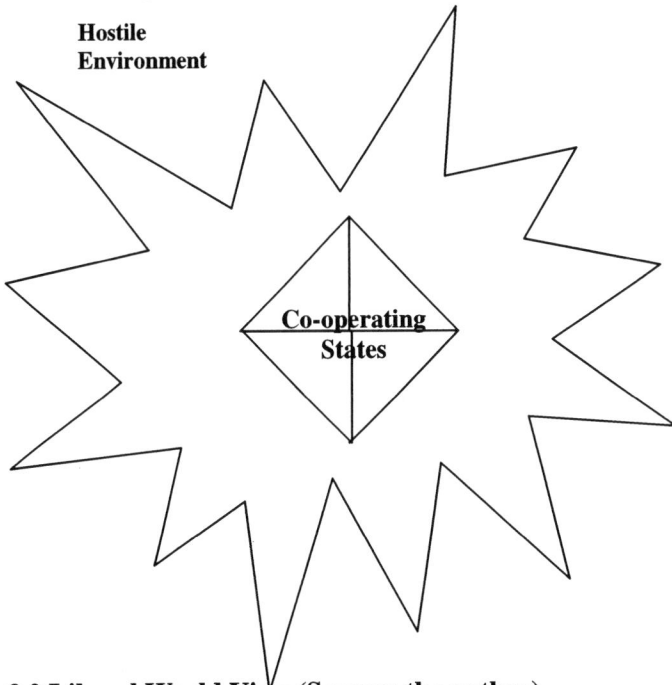

Hostile Environment

Co-operating States

3.2 Liberal World View (Source: the author)

Liberals are, however, divided (once again) over the method to achieve peaceful co-operation among states, and offer three alternative approaches: Liberal Internationalism, Liberal Idealism and Liberal Institutionalism.

Liberal Internationalism was a product of the Enlightenment, a reaction against the 'barbarity' of international politics at a time when domestic politics was on the verge of a new age of 'liberal' rights, citizenship and constitutionalism. The overriding belief was that reason could deliver freedom and justice in international relations. Immanuel Kant believed that *"the imperative to achieve peace was the transformation of individual consciousness, republican constitutionalism and a federal contract between states to abolish war"*. Jeremy Bentham advocated the creation of an international tribunal so that differences of opinion could be settled without recourse to war. While for Richard Cobden the 'natural order' had been corrupted by undemocratic state leaders and therefore the progress of freedom depended upon the maintenance of peace, the spread of commerce and the diffusion of education (Dunne 2001, pp.165-7).

Liberal Idealism, which flourished in the inter-war period, was motivated by a desire to prevent war, but sceptical that laissez-faire economic principles, such as free trade would deliver peace. J. A. Hobson argued that imperialism and the search for higher profits was in fact the primary cause of war, as it led capitalist countries into competition and conflict. While sharing with internationalists the belief that world public opinion could tame the interests of states, they believed that it was necessary to construct a new world order rather than rely on a return to 'natural order' to deliver peace. The fact that Britain and Germany had highly interdependent economies before the Great War, appeared to confirm the fatal flaw in the liberal internationalist association between interdependence, reason and peace. In the aftermath of the War, liberal thinking shifted toward this recognition that peace is not a natural condition, but one that must be constructed. Woodrow Wilson argued that peace could be achieved only with the creation of an international institution to regulate international anarchy, a belief that underpinned the notion of 'collective security' and the creation of the League of Nations. This idealism was the antithesis of realism because it was normative, asserting that scholarship should be about what ought to be, not just what is. It was largely discredited, however, when force reasserted itself and the League failed to avert the Second World War.

Liberal Institutionalism emerged to replace Idealism in the 1940s. While eschewing much of Idealism's normative prescriptions it did recognise the need to replace the League with another institution charged with responsibility for international peace and security. Central to the Institutionalist project in the post-war period was a belief in integration. The aim was to extend the range of collaboration among states so that the cost of withdrawing from co-operative efforts was greater than the advantages to be gained from going to war, a belief that became the driving force behind today's European Union. In the US, institutionalism manifested itself under the guise of pluralism, which recognised the increasing inter-connectedness between states and stressed the role of other international, or trans-national actors, such as business corporations and Non-governmental Organisations (NGOs) that existed alongside states. By the 1970s Liberal Institutionalism posed a significant challenge to realism through focusing on new actors and new patterns of interaction between states.

It will be obvious from the preceding discussion that liberalism is a broad church, and could promote either legitimising or project identities. It has tended, however, to support the former rather than the latter. Since the 1980s international relations has been dominated by a debate between Neo-realism and Neo-liberalism, the updated progeny of realism and liberal institutionalism, which borrows equally from realism and liberalism. They are both status quo perspectives, but for neo-liberals the question is how to promote and support co-operation in an anarchic and competitive international system, while for the neo-realists the key to survival is self-help. Neither, however, advances radical reform or the transformation of the international system. Allied to this has been the victory of economic liberalism over 'Keynsian' economics, and a diminishing role for the direct involvement of the state in stimulating economic demand. Instead the emphasis has shifted toward support for supply side measures, such as modernizing education.

In contrast to traditional education, modernizers stress the importance of national economic performance rather than military security, and therefore the role that education should play in supporting a state's business and industry. The need for applied knowledge and flexible skills, therefore, holds precedence over academic learning. Education, modernizers insist, must be responsive to the requirements of the market and develop habits of co-operation, teamwork and social skills (Ball op cit). On the one hand it is about transforming individuals, by elevating their education from the drudgery and conformity of mass schooling, but on the other it is about harnessing these individuals to the paramount needs of the state, in this case economic performance as opposed to security and social control. It is part of wider undertaking to transform society, for economic gain in this case, and can therefore be called a project identity. Nevertheless, it remains within the overall framework of the nation-state system competing in a hostile international system and therefore acts to further legitimise the state. This approach currently dominates the international system.

Project identity – critical theory and progressive education
The final approach emerges from critical theory and develops the concept of project identities, which Castells defines as ones in which *"social actors, on the basis of whichever cultural materials are available to them, build a new identity that redefines their position in society and, by*

doing so, seeks the transformation of the overall social structure" (Castells op cit p.8). Critical theory developed in the 1920s and 30s out of the intellectual traditions of Marxism, but was first articulated in 1937, in an article written by Max Horkheimer. In it he took issue with traditional theory (positivism) and asserted that it was incorrect to see the world as a set of facts waiting to be discovered, because facts could not be perceived independently of the social framework in which they occur. Critical theory, which he proposed as an alternative, saw facts as the product of specific social and historical frameworks, and by recognising this was able to reflect on the interests served by any particular theory.

Developing this theme in the context of international relations, Robert Cox, writing in the 1980s, made the observation that knowledge is always for someone and some purpose. He described traditional theories, which he termed problem-solving theories, as being *"geared to making the international system function more smoothly on the understanding that fundamental change is either impossible or improbable"*. Critical theory, on the other hand, *"searches for evidence of change on the assumption that present structures are unlikely to be reproduced indefinitely"* (Linklater 1998, p.281). Building on the work of Antonio Gramsci, Cox transported several of Gramsci's key concepts to the international arena, notably that of hegemony.

The key question of Gramsci's work was why had it proven so difficult to promote revolution in Western Europe. Where was the flaw in Marxist analysis? His answer revolved around the concept of hegemony, which is a conceptualisation of power, but broader and deeper than the traditional conception of military might. He adopted Machiavelli's view of power, which envisioned it as a Centaur, half man, half beast, a necessary combination of consent and coercion (Cox 1993, p.52). Marxists, like realists, had concentrated on the coercive powers of the state, ignoring the fact that power is maintained by consent as well as coercion. The hegemony of a state allows the moral, political and cultural values of the dominant group to become widely dispersed throughout society and to be accepted by subordinate groups and classes as their own. All this takes place through the institutions of civil society, which are *"the network of institutions and practices in society that enjoy some autonomy from the state, and through which groups and individuals organise, represent and express themselves to each other and the state"*. These include, for example, the media, the education system, churches and voluntary organisations, etc. (Hobden and Wyn-Jones 2001, pp.209-11). Herbert Marcuse, a leading light of early critical theory, described it as a 'one-dimensional' society, to which the vast majority simply cannot begin to conceive an alternative (Ibid p.215). An example would be the present widespread acceptance of neo-liberal policies, such as reduced state spending, privatisation and the promotion of free trade, which are advocated as vital in an increasingly competitive global environment. Gramsci proposed that society could be transformed only if the hegemonic position of the ruling class was successfully challenged, which entailed a 'counter-hegemonic' struggle in civil society, in which the prevailing hegemony is undermined, allowing an alternative to be constructed.

Cox has been enormously influential because he attacked the main assumptions of neo-realism, and criticized its hidden normative commitments. Rather than being an 'objective' theory, Cox exposed it as having a series of views about how states should be configured and how they should pursue their foreign policies. Neo-realism, therefore, typifies a traditional theory, in which theory is regarded as neutral and concerned only with uncovering pre-existing facts in an independent external world. In Cox's own words, it *"takes the world as it finds it, with the prevailing social and power relationships and the institutions into which they are organised, as the given framework for action"*. The aim is to make these relationships and institutions work smoothly by dealing effectively with sources of trouble. The general pattern of relationships is not called into question and the effect is to **legitimise** the existing order (Smith, S. p.235). This is not to suggest, however, that critical theory is neutral; on the contrary it is interested in social and political transformation and promotes progressive alternatives toward this end. For the purposes of this paper, two of these progressive alternatives are particularly relevant: the 'discourse ethics' of Habermas and Linklater's notion of political community.

Jurgen Habermas took issue with Marxism's emphasis on the importance of 'labour' for the structure of society and historical change, which he felt underestimated the role of 'interaction'. What was missing from their analysis was the recognition that emancipation required more than the destruction of class inequalities. *"The additional ingredient was progress in social communication and the radical democratisation of social, economic and political life"*, which led Habermas to develop what he calls 'discourse ethics' (Linklater 2001, p.146). Recognising that modern societies no longer have secure foundations for their ethical beliefs and are unlikely to find a single moral code upon which all human beings can agree, Habermas sought procedures which would make it possible for the exponents of different moralities to co-exist. 'Discourse ethics' was his solution. Its key requirement is that individuals must bring their different ethical positions before the *"tribunal of open discussion or dialogue"*. As Linklater explains, *"the point of open dialogue is to establish whether or not there is any consensus regarding the best moral argument. If there is no consensus – and consensus must never be forced – they must then negotiate a just compromise between their competing positions"* (Ibid p.147).

Dialogue, as Bill Williamson (2001 p.188) describes it, is 'a special form of communication... undertaken within a commitment to arrive at an agreed understanding of something.' For this to take place, however, a number of prior conditions must be met:

- Those engaged in it must respect one another's right to their opinions.
- They must share the same language (cooperative rather than conflictual, as opposed to sharing the English language for example).
- They must be aware of the logical principles of argument.
- They must have knowledge about the problem being discussed.
- They must be prepared to change their views if the argument and the evidence being examined justifies their doing so.

Borrowing from the work of Richard Devetak (2001, pp.173-4) and Bill Williamson, it is possible to identify three implications of 'discourse ethics' for the transformation of the international political system and the development of sustainable peace. First, the parameters for dialogue outlined above describe what Habermas called the 'ideal speech situation', in the absence of which communication is distorted. Despite describing an ideal situation it is still a powerful tool for understanding social relationships and institutions; it helps to identify the *"mechanisms of deceit, manipulation and ideological control through which the powerful can maintain their dominance"* (Williamson op cit). Second, by virtue of its inclusive and consent-orientated approach, it offers a democratic process for decision-making. Third, it offers a *"procedure for regulating violent conflict and arriving at resolutions which are acceptable to all affected parties"* (Devetak op cit p.174). In pursuit of the latter, Williamson uses the example of the conflict resolution work of Adam Curle, who emphasises that an acknowledgement of the way people perceive one another is vital in navigating a way out of conflict. People need to understand themselves and make sense of their experience of one another. Curle's peace workshops are a means to promote listening, self-reflection and joint analyses of complex problems of history, politics and identity (Williamson op cit pp.186-7).

Curle's work also highlights the other progressive alternative that I have referred to, that of 'political community' advocated by Andrew Linklater. Curle argues that emancipation is best understood in terms of the expansion of the moral boundaries of political community. In Curle's own words:

> *"Negative emotions are like a fist tightly closed around the heart. They imprison our consciousness within narrow confines of the self. But to be fully human our consciousness must expand, gradually embracing others, including all non-human others with whom we share the planet. It means losing the lonely sense of separation"* (Curle 1995 p.119).

In his work on political community, Linklater first analysed the way in which inequality and domination emanate from the type of political community associated with the sovereign state. He then went on to consider alternative forms of political community that promote 'human emancipation'. Modern political and ethical thought has been structured on the assumption that the state is the 'normal' form of political community and Linklater is particularly concerned with how this has allowed us to differentiate ethical obligations due to co-citizens from those due the rest of humanity. As Devetak explains, the problem with the nation-state is that as a 'limited moral community' it promotes exclusion, generating estrangement, injustice, insecurity and violent conflict between self-regarding states by imposing rigid boundaries between 'us' and 'them' (Devetak p.166). In other words, state borders act as an ethical boundary, beyond which at the very least our sense of duty and obligation is radically transformed and continues only in attenuated form. The goal, therefore, is to move toward a situation where our duties and obligations are the same toward non-citizens as they are toward fellow citizens.

There have of course been many positive developments in this regard in the post-Cold War environment, with increasing demands among citizens of affluent societies, for humanitarian intervention to alleviate suffering in states marred by civil conflicts and state terror. This desire to help, however, holds its own dangers and has led to accusations of cultural imperialism – the export of western values and institutions without regard to the wishes of the recipient nations. The solution, nevertheless, remains the same, to extend the sphere in which human beings treat each other as free and equal. Such a transformation is not going to happen overnight, but as Hobden and Wyn-Jones (2001) point out, an important element of critical theory is to identify and nurture tendencies that point toward emancipation.

Unsurprisingly, the approach to education which best exemplifies this approach is that which I have labelled 'progressive'. This is a contentious and misunderstood term, but for my purposes I focus upon the progressives' belief that education in its present form reinforces dominant interests, and instead citizens need to cultivate critical skills, moral questioning and an understanding of the functioning of modern, complex societies. Education should be responsive to the needs of individuals and the community, learner-centred, with an emphasis on co-operation and empowerment. The most distinguished exponent of such an approach is Paulo Freire, who wrote that, *"a deepened consciousness of their situation leads men to apprehend that situation as an historical reality susceptible of transformation"* (Freire 1996, p.58). He initiated a programme of emancipatory education in 1960s Brazil, which combined literacy training with political awareness. His pedagogy was built on three fundamental ideas: consciousness, dialogue and praxis (Meighan 1995). Consciousness described the process of *"learning to perceive social, political, and economic contradictions"*, dialogue was designed to deepen and develop this awareness, through reflection and articulation, and praxis was the ability *"to take action against the oppressive elements of reality"* (Freire op cit p.17).

Freire, like Miss Jean Brodie, criticised the 'banking concept' of education, in which the educator's role was to regulate the way the world 'entered' into the students. The teacher's task was to 'fill' the students by making deposits of information that they considered to constitute knowledge. Since this was a passive acceptance of the world by the students, education would make them more passive still, and adapt them to the world. As Freire explained, when *"translated into practice, this concept is well suited to the purposes of the oppressors, whose tranquillity rests on how well people fit the world the oppressors have created, and how little they question it"* (Ibid p.57). In terms of conflict resolution Freire's alternative of 'emancipatory education' fits exactly with the role ascribed to the 'educator' by Lederach, which is, to erase ignorance and raise awareness 'as to the nature of the unequal relationships and the need for addressing and restoring equity… among those experiencing the injustices. The crucial point is that this will inevitably lead to *"demands from the weaker party for change"* (Lederach op cit p.64). Freire's message, and that of the progressive approach in general, expressed through the notion of project identities, is that as people begin to transform themselves they begin to transform the world.

Peace education strategies
From a theoretical perspective it will be apparent that only project identities, with the support of critical theory and progressive forms of education, can lead us out of the 'circle of hate'. Liberal theory can offer an escape, particularly in its 'idealist' guise, yet in its present form it promotes a similar worldview to that of the realists, the primacy of the state, differing only over the methods to achieve its survival. Realists reject the very notion of transformation, while for liberals it extends no further than the present system. That is not to say that either discount the role of education in building peace, on the contrary education is seen as a useful

tool in suppressing dissent and ensuring conformity. Indeed, this may be the most appropriate use for education if a progressive approach were to prove ineffective. To judge if this is the case it is necessary to consider the practical application of educational theories to conflict resolution and building sustainable peace, and the peace education strategies on the far right of the model provide useful preliminary guidelines.

Although developed by Berlowitz (1994, pp.82-95) as ways to promote peace in US schools, they have wider application because the approaches employed are familiar to conflict resolution at the intra-state level (see Hutchinson 1996, p.253). In this case, explanation of the three approaches: peacekeeping, peacemaking and peacebuilding have been adapted from a presentation given by Ian Harris (2001).

"Traditionally", Harris writes, *"schools have relied upon* **peacekeeping** *responses to the problems of youth violence, trying to intimidate children from committing acts of violence by threatening them with severe punishments"*. He cites as examples, expulsion, metal detectors, weapon searches, security guards and police in schools. *"In conjunction with this peacekeeping approach"*, Harris continues, *"a* **peacemaking** *approach has been developed where teachers and psychologists have been teaching conflict resolution skills in school settings... peer mediation programmes try to resolve conflicts between parties... they use a third party, mediator, to help the parties resolve their differences"*. The third approach is **peacebuilding,** *"that tries to teach youth how to live peacefully on this planet. Peacebuilding assumes that the problems of violence reside in the culture surrounding youth. The goal is to give young people insights into the sources of this violence and empower them to avoid and transform it"*. The three approaches sit surprisingly well at the end of the theoretical model and provide a helpful introduction to the practical role of education.

Chapter four

This side of the grave: Britain – a pre-conflict case study

Upon the education of the people of this country the fate of this country depends.

Benjamin Disraeli, (Hansard 11 March 1873)

To talk of the United Kingdom as a state in conflict in relation to the circle of hate may sound rather odd, notwithstanding over thirty years of violence in Northern Ireland and occasional bombing on the mainland.   The Second World War ended over fifty years ago, we are no longer involved in post-colonial wars and even the battle for the Falklands is two decades distant.   Furthermore, these were either 'traditional' inter-state conflicts or counter-insurgency operations many miles from Britain's shores. The last intra-state conflict in Britain was surely the Jacobite Rebellion of 1745-6 and the English Civil War a hundred years before that.   We have since avoided a French-style revolution in the aftermath of 1789, and the revolutions that shook Europe in the late 1840s also passed us by.

Yet what of the Luddite disturbances in 1811 and their agricultural equivalent the 'Swing' riots in 1831, the Chartist riots in 1839, the General Strike of 1926, the miners' strike 1984-5, the race riots of the 1980s, the poll tax riots of 1989 and more recently the May Day riots in London and ethnic rioting in Bradford?   These events in Britain and the 'Troubles' in Northern Ireland raise two questions: first, how do you define a state in conflict; and second, is a state in conflict if the associated violence disfigures only a portion of the country, leaving the majority of the population largely untouched and, it could be said, largely unmoved?   Full answers are well beyond the scope of this book, but it can be safely said that conflict has more faces than its traditional military guise and within any nation-state a number of 'circles of hate' may be revolving at the same time, albeit at different rates.

Conflict in Britain and Europe
Violent conflict in Britain has broadly followed trends observable internationally, in that clashes fuelled by ideology, (workers versus the ruling classes), perhaps last seen during the miners' strike in the 1980s, have declined along with the Cold War and the focus has shifted to dealing with resistance identities. In Britain's case: increasing drug-use and crime (including rioting), and inter-ethnic violence. The government's response has been wide-ranging and has included efforts to address truancy and anti-social behaviour in schools, through what Harris has described as peacekeeping and peacebuilding approaches (see end of last chapter). In the case of the former, police officers are to be based in four hundred of England's worst affected schools (Smithers 30 April 2002), which is noteworthy in itself, but perhaps more notable is the introduction of citizenship education in the school curriculum. (The introduction of Citizenship Education is restricted to England and Wales. Scotland and Northern Ireland have essentially separate educational systems, under the control of their own governing bodies.)

It is notable for two reasons: firstly Britain has been an exception in that it has previously omitted social and civic education from the compulsory core of its curriculum. In East Asian States a central place is reserved for learning 'which encourages moral understanding and which promotes social cohesion through appreciation of national traditions and goals and the meaning of citizenship (Green 1997, p.49). Among European nations Britain has been an exception, not seeing school as a *"major instrument in the forging of national identity"* (Ibid p.94). Even in Scotland citizenship education is well established through modern and environmental studies (Kerr 1998 p.2). English and Welsh education has instead emphasised the *"personal development of the individual pupil over the collective educational needs of society"* (Green op cit p.95).

Secondly, with the rise of the neo-liberal economics, education has become more closely integrated with the economy in the widely held belief that the nation has little chance of developing a sound post-industrial economy unless it has a well-educated workforce. As Andy Green makes clear, *"in the advanced states ... with the possible exception of Japan ... citizen formation has given way to skills formation, nation building to national economic competitiveness"* (Ibid p.4). Britain is therefore rejecting its own traditions and the international trend. The question is why?

According to J. Esteve, cited by Harber (2002 p.9), *"in many societies the authority mechanisms that schools have traditionally relied on to enforce control and conformity no longer work as effectively as they did and pupils increasingly challenge control and imposition in violent ways as schools have not yet found a satisfactory way to organise a peaceful social environment that offers respect to everyone: staff and pupils".* In the opinion of David Kerr, Professional Officer to the advisory group on 'Education for Citizenship and the teaching of Democracy in Schools' (known as the Crick Report) citizenship has been introduced to the curriculum in response to *"the wider social and political context of rapidly changing relationships between the individual and the government and the decline in traditional forms of civic cohesion* (what has been termed a 'democratic deficit'). *But perhaps the most pressing factor is the worrying signs of alienation and cynicism among young people about public life and participation, leading to their possible disconnection and disengagement from it"* (Kerr op cit pp.2-3).

Catherine Larkin (2001 p.15), following research on the
Crick Report, is more direct, believing that:

> *"the need for citizenship education seems to be a*
> *negative, almost fearful one, tinged with what appears*
> *to be fear for the very foundations of British*
> *democracy.   There are seeming concerns that an*
> *entire generation has opted out of politics and*
> *engaged citizenship.   There are further concerns*
> *about the measures of widespread anti-social*
> *disengagedness spanning from a lack of interest in*
> *political issues, low voting records and growing*
> *disregard for the mechanisms of democracy, to*
> *habitual drug taking, premeditated violence and*
> *general lawlessness. The problems of the society have*
> *been laid squarely at the feet of young people and the*
> *'solution' put forward is the provision of citizenship*
> *education in schools".*

The fears of the British government can only have increased
in 2001 following events in France, where voter apathy led
to a far-right candidate, espousing xenophobic and
nationalist policies, contesting the final stage of the
presidential election. Nor is this an isolated incident, across
Western Europe far-right parties have made electoral gains.
The most striking was two years previously in Austria,
where Jorg Haider's right-wing Freedom Party came to
power in a coalition with a centre-right party.

More recently in Holland the party of the late Pim Fortuyn
(who significantly was shot dead for his views) joined the
coalition government, ousting more moderate rivals. As
Stephen Castle put it, writing in *The Independent*, they all
"swim in a similar pool of disenchantment, exploiting the
same fear of crime, insecurity, worries over globalisation
and – most of all – concern about immigration" (23 April
2002).   The same destructively negative identities
considered in Chapter Two. Britain's own far-right party,
the British National Party (BNP), is not a threat nationally,
but it does have significant areas of local strength. The East

End of London is a traditional area of support, but it has recently made strong gains in the north. Two years ago the party did not put up a single candidate in Burnley, but following the local elections in 2003 it is now the official opposition on the local council.

The case should not be overstated, however. While acknowledging that the recent victories of the far-right, the violence perpetrated against synagogues and the murder of Pim Fortuyn, give the impression that *"violence and racism might become the Europe's new norm"*, the *Economist* does not believe that Europe is 'irredeemable' (11 April 2002 pp.11-12). In Larkin's opinion, citizenship education, though not a panacea for social problems, will, if given adequate resources and support by both the government and individual schools, play a positive role in countering these trends (Op cit p.1). She is not alone. When asked by the Sunday Times, in the aftermath of 11 September, *"How can we tackle the roots of Islamic extremism among young people, especially in this country?"* Professor Adam Roberts replied thus:

> *"Education is crucial – both for good and for evil. Generally terrorist ideas flourish where political culture is low, where there is a ghetto mentality rather than a give-and-take in political ideas, and where education in politics, history and international relations is weak. A key part of the response to terrorism has to be to raise the level of political education, **including in the UK** (emphasis added). Both constitutional politics and non-violent forms of struggle need to be actively promoted as better and more ethical means of achieving political and economic ends"* (7 Oct 2001).

The introduction of citizenship education in England and Wales is a welcome recognition that education is more than just a tool of the economy. Its success, however, in promoting conflict resolution and sustainable peace depends upon its content and practical application in schools.

Citizenship education in England and Wales

From September 2001 citizenship education became a
statutory part of the national curriculum for Key Stages 3
and 4 (it is already taught to younger children on a non-
statutory basis). Citizenship is explained on the Department
for   Education   and   Employment   (DfEE)   website.
Programmes of study set out what pupils should be taught,
and attainment targets set out the expected standards of
pupils performance. It is, however, for individual schools to
choose how they organise their school curriculum to include
the programmes of study in order to meet the attainment
targets.

These targets are defined on the website as the 'knowledge,
skills and understanding that pupils of different abilities and
maturities are expected to have by the end of the key stage'
(the specific targets for Key Stages 3 and 4 are attached at
Appendices 1 & 2). In addition it is an inter-disciplinary
subject and therefore, rather than being taught as a discrete
subject, can be integrated across the entire curriculum. The
government's aspiration is for it to promote the following:

- Spiritual development. Through fostering pupils'
  awareness and understanding of meaning and
  purpose in life and of differing values in human
  society.
- Moral   development.   Through   helping   pupils
  develop a critical appreciation of issues of right
  and wrong, justice, fairness, rights and obligations
  in society.
- Social   development.   Through   helping   pupils
  acquire the understanding and skills needed to
  become responsible and effective members of
  society.
- Cultural development. Through helping pupils
  understand the nature and role of the different
  groups to which they belong, and promoting
  respect for diversity and difference.

It is important to note that government guidance states that children should learn not only through formal lessons, but also through active participation in class and as responsible citizens. Both aspects will be included in inspection reports by the Office for Standards in Education (OFSTED).

Working from Clive Harber's premise, as presented in Chapter One, that *"the twin fundamental goals of education should be peace and democracy"*, it is necessary to assess the role of citizenship education in this regard and therefore to compare its aspirations against a suitable benchmark. None seems more appropriate than UN Resolution A/RES/53/243, *Declaration and Programme of Action on a Culture of Peace*, which it defines as, *"a set of values, attitudes, modes of behaviour and ways of life that reject violence and prevent conflicts by tackling their root causes to solve problems through dialogue and negotiation among individuals, groups and nations"* (UNESCO website). For this to prevail the UN proposes that we need to *"foster a culture of peace through education by revising the educational curricula to promote qualitative values, attitudes and behaviours of a culture of peace, including peaceful conflict-resolution, dialogue, consensus-building and active non-violence"*. Furthermore, such an educational approach should be geared to:

- Promoting sustainable economic and social development
- Promoting respect for all human rights
- Ensuring equality between women and men
- Fostering democratic participation
- Advancing understanding, tolerance and solidarity
- Supporting participatory communication and the free flow of information and knowledge
- Promoting international peace and security

(The full text is at Appendix 3)

Comparing the goals of citizenship education in England and Wales (Appendices 1 & 2) with the UN 'Culture of Peace'

(Appendix 3) it is apparent that the goals of citizenship education meet many of the criteria for the UN's Culture of Peace, specifically the promotion of democracy, human rights, sustainable development, equality, understanding and tolerance, and participatory communication. There is, however, a crucial omission, namely the explicit promotion of a culture of peace and non-violence, which seems odd given the otherwise close parallels. While acknowledging that the inculcation of democratic values in our children from this September onward is not guaranteed to succeed, improving democracy is nevertheless a stated aim of citizenship education and only time will tell if it is at all successful. Given the aim of this book, however, it is the failure to include the promotion of peace and non-violence that will be investigated.

Peace education and promotion of non-violence
The omission of peace education and the promotion of non-violence become explicable if we return to the theoretical discourses presented in chapter three and recognise that citizenship education in England and Wales is a product of the dominant liberal discourse. While recognising the need to foster co-operation rather than conflict within and among states, the liberal discourse retains the realist belief in an anarchic international environment, where military power remains the ultimate arbiter. Consequently, references to the promotion of peace and non-violence have presumably been ignored as nonsensical or irrelevant.

Yet if we are to have even a chance of escaping the 'circle of hate' surely non-violent alternatives to conflict resolution must be offered to children. In the first place, however, it is necessary to challenge the basic assumption that military power is the ultimate arbiter.

This militaristic belief is based upon the premise that human beings are by nature violent, aggressive and competitive and the corollary assumption that social order must therefore be maintained by force and power. While the logic, however, is impeccable it is based upon an debatable premise. The belief that human beings are by nature violent is widely contested. The *Seville Statement on Violence*, drawn up in 1986 by scholars of the relevant sciences from around the world, and subsequently adopted by UNESCO on 16 November 1989, put forward five propositions challenging the belief that violence in humans is genetic. Each proposition began with the statement, 'It is scientifically incorrect to say that:

- We have inherited a tendency to make war from our animal ancestors
- War or any other violent behaviour is genetically programmed into our human nature
- In the course of human evolution there has been a selection for aggressive behaviour more than other kinds of behaviour
- Humans have a 'violent brain'.
- War is caused by 'instinct' or any single motivation

They concluded that: *"just as wars begin in the minds of men, so peace also begins in our minds. The same species who invented war is capable of inventing peace"* (Seville Statement on Violence, Spain 1986 – UNESCO website).

More recent support for this statement can be drawn from scientists in the aftermath of 11 September. Dr David Sloan-Wilson, Professor of Biology at the State University of New York, while acknowledging that, *"altruism is practiced within your group, and often turned off toward members of other groups"*, did not see conflict as inevitable, *"it's been shown"*, he continued, *"that where people place the boundary between 'us' and 'them' is extremely flexible. It's possible to widen the moral circle, and I'm optimistic enough to believe it can be done on a worldwide scale"*.

Dr James Moore concurred, *"the original horrific act notwithstanding, the overall picture to come out about human nature is wonderful. For every 50 people making bomb threats to mosques, there are 500,000 people behaving just the way we hoped they would, with empathy and expressions of grief"* (*Guardian* 22 September 2001). Professor Richard Dawkins, speaking five months later, observed that *"although we are products of Darwinianism we are not slaves to it. Using the large brains that Darwinian natural selection has given us, it is possible to fashion new values that contradict Darwinian values"* (Royal Institution Lecture). The conclusion is, as Robert Hinde points out, that while *"humans are certainly capable of aggression... it is not inevitable that they should be aggressive. In the course of evolution, natural selection has ensured that individuals are born with the potentials to behave not only aggressively, but also co-operatively, acquisitively, assertively, altruistically and in many other ways"* (1990, p.172).

The aim of peace education is to develop the positive potential of human beings, as a counter to the negative and pessimistic image of human nature purveyed by militarism. It is an attempt to create a new way of perceiving the world. As Birgit Brock-Utne points out, however, *"when history is taught as a series of wars and natural science is taught without taking ecological and human consequences into account, such teaching naturally influences the attitudes and norms that are being transmitted"* (1988 p.90). She believes that *"as history is presently taught, important phenomena, such as the effective use of non-violence and the important role of women in society, are rendered invisible, hidden, forgotten"* (Ibid p.84).

Robert Hinde argues that history has given war *"an honourable status... and much of the history that is taught is the history of wars"*. That is not to denigrate the self-sacrifice of the men and women who have suffered and died in war, but he asks us to *"see that other traditions are possible"*. He gives the examples of Switzerland and Sweden, both with militaristic traditions, but who have chosen to change their orientation (op cit p.80).

There is a considerable history of successful non-violent approaches to conflict, but India's Movement for Self-Rule, the American Civil Rights Campaign and South Africa's Campaign Against Apartheid tend to be ignored in the school history curriculum. Brock-Utne believes that *"it is important to teach non-violent solutions to conflict at all levels of formal schooling... so that non-violent methods become the normal means of conflict resolution"* (op cit p.94). The aim is not to suggest to children that conflict is abnormal, on the contrary, like the search for identity, it is a normal and natural part of life, but it is to suggest that conflict need not lead automatically to a violent solution.

It is not enough, however, just to tell children that there is an alternative to violent conflict and furnish them with historical examples, to paraphrase Harber, like democratic values and behaviours, non-violent conflict resolution is learned as much by experience as by hearing or reading about it (2002). Brock-Utne believes that *"the success of peace education can perhaps be judged more by the way pupils behave towards one another in the schoolyard and the classroom than by the amount of learning they are able to reproduce about the arms race or disarmament"* (op cit p.95).

Such an approach is already offered by the 'Sintra Plan of Action' (mentioned above), which argues that *"the principles and practices of peace and non-violence should be integrated into every aspect of curriculum, pedagogy and activities, including the very organisational and decision-making structure of the educational institution. These include co-operative learning, dialogue, intercultural understanding, mediation and conflict-resolution strategies"* (p.2).

Interestingly, though not yet adopted by the Government, elements of this practical approach can be observed in an increasing number of schools in England and Wales, in the form of peer support schemes. Professor Helen Cowie, who has observed the phenomena for over a decade, has seen the numbers of such schemes increase in the last four years from only sixty projects, to a situation today where most schools have such programmes.

In Kingsbury High School, a mixed comprehensive in north London, there is a peer support project, known as 'Connect', *"in which pupils of various ages volunteer to be trained to give educational and emotional support and friendship to their fellows. The help ranges from one-to-one aid for bullies and bullied, assertiveness training, a break-time drop-in centre for those on their own, playground befriending, and buddying for new pupils, to paired reading and a homework club.' Not only does this scheme offer support to those children in need, but it also helps build the confidence and life-skills of those who offer their help. Significantly, in Kingsbury High School, 'the number of angry conflicts in the playground has reduced dramatically"* (*Independent* 21 Feb 2002).

Internationally an increasing number of schools are implementing peer mediation schemes to help resolve conflict (what Harris describes as a 'peacemaking' approach). *"The challenge"*, according to Catherine Larkin, *"is to teach people how to deal constructively with conflict and hopefully in a way that will transform the participants and teach them something not only about the other person's perspective but also about their own"* (2001, pp.10-11).

Larkin explains the peer mediation scheme by focusing on the role of the mediator, whom she describes as an impartial third party who provides a context in which conflicting parties have an opportunity to speak and be heard. He or she may offer suggestions for a possible outcome, but will leave the final resolution entirely in the hands of the conflicting parties themselves. The actual process of mediation varies depending upon the setting, but Larkin has observed the following procedure to be most useful in the school setting:

1. Each disputing party explains their side (perception)

of the conflict, without interruption, to the mediator and the other party.

2. The parties are then encouraged by the mediator to consider not only on the actual problem that brought about the conflict, but also 'the reasons that they feel aggrieved by the dispute. Thus the 'focus is on the needs of the parties rather than their stated positions.'

3. The mediator attempts to engage the parties in a **constructive dialogue** (emphasis added) where the conflict is viewed as a common problem whose resolution will be of benefit to both parties. Crucially the disputants are encouraged to deal with the problem not the person. The process is designed to increase empathy between the parties and to lead them to understand both sides of the problem, to see that many problems are not based so much on 'truth' as on 'perceptions', and that 'an appreciation of those perceptions may lead the parties to a greater chance of resolution.'

4. The mediator then assists the parties to consider options for a mutually beneficial resolution of the conflict (Ibid pp.11- 12).

Larkin concludes that *"for students who learn the elemental skills of mediation – such as active listening, empathy, creativity, and responsibility for their own conflict and decisions – peace education is already well underway.' Furthermore, 'all the listed essential elements to be attained through citizenship education may be found in the process of peace education through mediation and positive conflict resolution"* (Ibid pp.12-13).

Concluding observations
This chapter has reflected on the British Government's attempts to address the problems of political disengagement and the growth of resistance identities among its citizens. It is acknowledged that the introduction of citizenship education may well be a step in the right direction as it

meets many of the criteria laid down by the UN as prerequisites for the development of a culture of peace.

The exclusion of peace education itself, however, is a regrettable omission. Not only does peace education offer an alternative to false militaristic logic and the dominance of violent conflict resolution in school history curricula, but its practical application also meets the stated aims of citizenship education. Nevertheless, positive local initiatives such as peer support and peer mediation schemes are gaining ground and if adopted by the Government would help address many of their concerns and contribute toward sustainable peace.

Chapter five

The far side of revenge: Northern Ireland – a post-conflict case study

> *You've got to be taught to hate and fear*
> *You've got to be taught from year to year*
> *It's got to be drummed in your dear little ear*
> *You've got to be carefully taught*
>
> *You've got to be taught to be afraid*
> *Of people whose eyes are oddly made*
> *And people whose skin is a different shade*
> *You've got to be carefully taught*
>
> *You've got to be taught before it's too late*
> *Before you are six or seven or eight*
> *To hate all the people your relatives hate*
> *You've got to be carefully taught*
> *You've got to be carefully taught.*
>
> (Rodgers and Hammerstein, *You've got to be carefully taught*,
> South Pacific 1949)

Any attempt to understand the role of education in schools in resolving the Northern Ireland conflict must first consider the environment in which children presently live, an environment that does in many cases teach them to hate 'all the people their relatives hate'. Despite recognition in the 1998 Good Friday Agreement that *"an essential aspect of the reconciliation process is the promotion of a culture of tolerance at every level of society, including initiatives to facilitate and encourage integrated education and mixed housing"*, a recent survey of 4,800 households conducted under the guidance of Dr Peter Shirlow, a senior lecturer in Geography at the University of Ulster, found that segregation between adjoining Catholic and Protestant communities in inner city Belfast had actually increased since the Agreement.

Analysis of the unpublished 2001 census revealed that while in 1991 63% of people lived in areas that were at least 90% Catholic or 90% Protestant, by 2001 this figure had risen to 66%. Figures from the Northern Ireland Housing Executive confirmed the trend, showing that in the second half of the 1991 – 2001 census period twice as many families asked to be moved to areas dominated by a particular denomination, often blaming their decision to move on intimidation (*The Independent* 4 Jan 2002).

What is most striking, however, are the findings that identify teenagers as the most sectarian age group, those who would have been in primary school at the time of the IRA and loyalist ceasefires, which preceded the Agreement (*Observer*, internet edition, 23 Sep 2001). Equally alarming is the statistic that 68% of 18 to 25 year-olds, who would have been in secondary school over the same period, have never had a meaningful conversation with anyone from the other community (Op cit *The Independent*). Dr Shirlow acknowledged that the phenomenon of growing segregation was largely confined to inner city Belfast (in suburban and rural areas people were integrating more), but increasing sectarianism could also be seen in towns such as Portadown, Lurgan and Carrickfergus.

The conclusion, in the words of David McKittrick, Northern Ireland correspondent for *The Independent*, appears to be that while the Good Friday Agreement *"commends reconciliation and initiatives to promote integrated education and mixed housing. The devolved government has not, however, made this a high priority ... partly because there is no big demand for integration in housing or schools."* In the *"sectarian cockpit of North Belfast ... the demand is not for integration but for peacelines" (The Independent* 4 Jan 2002).

Children as guardians of the sectarian tradition
The above findings make the words of Johnston McMaster all the more prescient. In 1993 he wrote that, *"it is all too easy for the Churches to make the generalised statement or assumption that young people are anti-sectarian and, if given the chance, will cross the divides and build a new community ... it ignores the fact that a significant number of young people are, in fact, guardians of the sectarian tradition"* (1993, p.3). McMaster presents a bleak picture of a tradition that dates back to at least the mid-nineteenth century, when children were acknowledged to have played a leading role in street disturbances.

Government reports of rioting in Belfast during the 1850s and 60s revealed that young people between ten and sixteen years of age often instigated riots and that similar patterns were evident in Derry. In the 1980s adolescent gangs continued the tradition as they patrolled and defended sectarian territorial boundaries (Ibid p.8). More recently young people have been both the victims and perpetrators of street violence during the disturbances surrounding Holy Cross Primary School in the autumn of 2001, which were re-ignited the following January by threats to children and staff at schools of both denominations, in north and west Belfast.

The Catholic pupils of Holy Cross, which is unfortunately located in a loyalist area, due to the demographic shifts mentioned above, actually bore the brunt of the local residents' wider grievances over alleged intimidation. Significantly, however, secondary schoolgirls were to be seen beside their protesting parents blowing whistles on the third morning of the Holy Cross protests (O'Connor *The Independent* 9 Sep 2001 p.4), and youths were prominent in the disturbances that led to Protestant children being ferried to their homes in the Shankhill Road district by police Land Rovers (McKittrick *The Independent* 11 Jan 2001).

McMasters believes that the present 'troubles' have seen increasing 'street politicisation' of young people through wall murals and paramilitary graffiti. In Loyalist areas kerbs are painted red, white and blue, while in Republican areas kerbs are painted green, white and orange. In particular he cites the wall murals, which *"accompanied by slogans provide insight into the street politicisation of young people. They express perceptions, interpretations of political history and ideology ...* [which in turn] *provide visual aids for the political education of young people"* (Op cit p.9).

Joseph Liechty and Cecelia Clegg, authors of *Moving Beyond Sectarianism*, agree, *"When ... murals carry evidence of threat, the desire for domination, or inappropriately quoted biblical texts, they become potent means for hardening the boundaries between groups. Simultaneously, they can act to raise both fear in the other and inflamed passions in their own community"* (2001, p.131).

The sad fact is that every generation since the mid-nineteenth century has either directly experienced serious sectarian conflict or inherited stories concerning such strife from parents. As Desmond Bell points out, *"A vivid popular memory of past clashes – their form, location and outcome – has been transmitted from generation to generation, giving renewed saliency in every fresh outbreak of violence"* (1990, p.79).

Many young people do not choose, or are unable, to break with their parents views and therefore *"on each side of the sectarian divide in contemporary Northern Ireland it is the teenage young who are centrally involved in the celebration of heritage"* (Ibid p.9). Those proposing educational remedies must also recognise that education itself has played a significant role in fostering the opposing traditions; the distinctive character of the education system in Northern Ireland is one of segregation.

5.1 – Republican Wall Mural, The Bogside, Derry
(Source: the author)

5.2 – Loyalist Wall Mural, Andersontown Road, Belfast (Source: the author)

As Fionnuala O'Connor observes, *"for most parents, separate education is not a conscious choice but part of the fabric of their lives"* (Op cit).   In Frank Wright's opinion; *"conflicts over educational systems were the beginning of many or perhaps most modern European national conflicts".* When minority groups reached a position from which to organise behind their own middle class, ascendant groups would try to oppose this by obstructing the minorities' efforts to control the education of their own children.

In the case of Ireland, *"defending Catholic education became a sacred duty for Irish nationalists ... because attacking Catholic education had always been seen as a way of uprooting Irishness"* (1991, p.23).   At present there are three government-supported educational initiatives in Northern Ireland designed to encourage reconciliation: integrated education, education for mutual understanding and the closely associated cross-community contact scheme. Given the historical nature of the sectarian divide, however, there seems little point in addressing these schemes directly without some knowledge of their historical development.

The education system in Northern Ireland

Before the 1780s Catholics in Ireland were subject to the Penal Laws, which included a ban on education, to prevent the emergence of a Catholic middle class and ensure that they remained 'hewers of wood and drawers of water.' Any education for Catholics that did exist, therefore, was conducted in illegal 'hedge' schools, which only became legal after the Penal Laws slackened following Catholic Ireland's failure to support the 1745 Jacobite rebellion. Education was then largely uncontested until controversies in their 'modern' form emerged around 1820, when, under the so-called 'Second Reformation', attempts were made by the Protestant hierarchy to ensure that education in Ireland led to the assimilation of Catholics.

This was challenged by Catholics and ultimately by the new Liberal government at Westminster, who recognised the necessity of providing an educational system that would meet Catholic fears about proselytising. The new National Education system, created by an Act of Parliament in 1833, was the first attempt to provide a non-denominational, essentially integrated education system in Ireland, which was described as 'mixed secular and separate religious instruction'. There was a tendency, however, for people to support integrated education most keenly when they thought their 'side' would gain from it. Protestant leaders favoured mixed education because they saw it as a way of breaking the cohesion of the Catholic community, while the Catholic Church demanded denominational education to counter this threat. The result was that schools became increasingly segregated. While the government, through its financial support, retained some control over the curriculum, the churches controlled their management, the employment of teaching staff and the provision of religious education.

At Partition, almost a century later, Northern Ireland inherited this pattern of schooling. Although there was a desire in some quarters to establish a unified education system for the new state which would be acceptable to Catholics and Protestants, Unionists and Nationalists, the bitterness and recrimination which marked the early years of Northern Ireland's existence made it impossible. Schools formerly controlled by the Protestant churches were transferred to the state and became 'controlled' schools, legally non-denominational but in practice Protestant.

The Catholic Church on the other hand, unable to reach a satisfactory agreement over transfer, decided to operate its schools independently. These became known as 'maintained' schools. Both 'controlled' and 'maintained' schools essentially provided primary education, though up to the age of fourteen in some cases. Secondary education at this time was limited, by both fees and selection, to that provided by grammar schools, which were referred to as 'voluntary' schools. These, though funded and managed under different arrangements, were still identifiably Catholic or Protestant.

Progress, stimulated in the main by Britain, was made in the aftermath of the Second World War. The 1947 Education Act, passed by the Stormont Parliament, was strongly influenced by the debate surrounding the 1944 Education Act in Great Britain. The 1947 Act increased funding for Catholic maintained schools, raised the school leaving age and set up 'controlled' and 'maintained' secondary schools so that all pupils were able to move at the age of eleven from a primary to a secondary school, without relying on fee-paying grammar schools. The segregation of schools, however, was unaffected.

As Fraser and Morgan (1999) point out, the essential features of Northern Ireland's dual system of education and the clear separation of the two major denominationally based elements remained unchanged. Even the moves to

ameliorate relations between the two communities during the
Premiership of Captain Terence O'Neill, however tentative,
had little effect upon education, which remained a clear and
reliable marker of community affiliation.   Nor did the
protests and violence of the late 1960s initially affect
education.   Those working in schools saw them
predominantly as 'oases of calm and security'.   Despite
sensing that segregated schooling compounded the region's
social and political divisions, there was still a far stronger
conviction that separate education was the only way to
ensure that schools respected the values of the children's
families.   It was only as analysis of the causes of the
'troubles' developed that the negative perception of separate
schooling gained ground.

Gradually the dual education system came to be seen as a
*"major element in a segregated social system, which
produced Protestants and Catholics with few contacts
outside their own section of the community"* (Fraser &
Morgan op cit p.7).   It therefore appeared straightforward to
claim that this would lead to stereotyped perceptions and
factual inaccuracies, which would in turn affect their adult
attitudes and behaviour.   The logical conclusion, as Mo
Mowlam later observed, was that *"if people can grow up
together and study together they are much more likely to be
able to live together"* (*The Independent* 9 Sep 2001).   Some
commentators, however, went further, claiming *that "not
only did schools separate children from Catholic and
Protestant backgrounds, they also transmitted the
oppositional elements in the cultures of the two groups
through the hidden curriculum and possibly more overtly
through the teaching of subjects such as history"* (Ibid).

This belief is widely contested, particularly by the respective
church hierarchies, and illustrates a central difficulty.
*"Unless people who distrust each other have some shared
trust in an authority above them both, the management of
that distrust can be exceedingly difficult.   Separate systems
of education have often been a way of making distrust*

between national communities manageable, and crucially for Catholics it has been a means of achieving social parity with Protestants" (Wright op cit p.5). In other words, legitimisation of the status quo has strong support among a population, who, by and large, feel safe within their own communities and at best have little interest in the other community.

Nevertheless, three broad initiatives for change have emerged. In the first place two approaches, under the broad banner of education for mutual understanding, designed to be incorporated in the existing segregated system, which include cross community programmes (with the aim of encouraging contact between Catholic and Protestant pupils) and the introduction of community relations material to the curriculum. The third initiative, on the other hand, is more radical and has attempted to change the structure of the education system to make it easier for Catholics and Protestants to be educated together. It was this latter approach that led to the emergence of integrated education in its present form.

Integrated education
The Northern Ireland Council for Integrated Education (NICIE) describe integrated education as:

> *"The bringing together in one school of pupils, staff and governors, in roughly equal numbers, from both Protestant and Catholic traditions. It is about cultivating the individual's self-respect and therefore respect for other people and other cultures. Integrated education means bringing children up to live as adults in a pluralist society, recognising what they hold in common as well as what separates them, and accepting both."*

The creation of integrated schools is widely regarded as the major development in Northern Irish education over the past two decades. It emerged from the efforts of the pressure group *All Children Together* (ACT), formed by parents from both communities in 1974, which successfully lobbied for legislation that would allow existing state schools to become integrated. The Dunleath Act of 1978 offered denominational schools the opportunity to take representatives of the 'other' community onto their Boards of Governors, which, it was hoped, would lead to schools becoming integrated. The Act was only invoked once, however, in order to save a school from closure, and in frustration ACT eventually decided to establish an integrated school of their own. The expectation was that this would encourage other schools to adopt integration as originally intended.

Lagan College opened in Belfast in 1981, with a charter prohibiting Catholic/Protestant enrolment drifting beyond 40:60/60:40 ratios. Three more integrated schools were created in 1985, establishing a pattern whereby at least one or two integrated schools have been created each year since (Smith, A 1999 p.8). By September 2002 there were 47 integrated schools - 18 Secondary Level Colleges, and 29 Primary Schools. In addition there are 13 Integrated Nursery Schools, most of which are linked to Primary schools. In total over 14,000 pupils attend integrated schools, (about 4% of the school population), and according to Fraser and Morgan, *"there is now an integrated primary school in almost every major population centre and although the travelling distances are considerable in some areas most parents now have the possibility of selecting an integrated primary school for their child"* (op cit p.14).

The growth of integrated education during the 1980s, however, was hindered by a lack of finance. Under Department for Education Northern Ireland (DENI) policy, schools could not receive government funding until they had proven their viability, through acceptable enrolment figures and evidence of pre-school children on a waiting list. As a result the initial set up had to be funded and managed by private individuals with the support of grants and loans from charitable foundations.

The situation only improved with the passage of the Education Reform (NI) Order in 1989. In part, like the 1947 Act, it reflected developments in education policy in Britain (in this case the 1988 Education Act for England and Wales) but it also focused on issues peculiar to Northern Ireland. Specifically, it introduced new procedures for approving and funding integrated schools. This was particularly significant because it promised quicker recognition of integrated schools, thereby reducing private funding, but crucially it acknowledged integrated schools as an established part of the education system.

The difficulty now facing the integrated schools sector is that while it commands only 4% of pupil enrolment in Northern Ireland, a remarkable achievement but short of its ideal aspirations, it is large enough to be seen by the denominational schools as competing for funding and resources.   As a result, while Catholic and Protestant denominational schools accept the need for anti-sectarian material in the curriculum, and of extending links between their two sectors, they object to the allocation of resources to integrated schools.   Some, both within and outside of government, argue that the integration of schools should be pursued as a primary aim of educational policy, despite the fact that this would undermine parental choice, the bedrock of current educational policy in the UK and a fundamental aim of the founders of integrated education.

Together with religiously balanced enrolment and the establishment of a distinctive ethos in which different religious and cultural traditions are respected, a key principle of the management structures of integrated schools has been to encourage the active involvement of parents at all stages in the school's development. Forcing parents to send their children to integrated schools would destroy this principle. As Frank Wright points out, the *"difficulties involved in respecting each other's tradition, whether in the syllabus, the style of teaching, the use of symbols and so on ... are resolved by parents and teachers together ... if instead children are pushed together most of the old problems which led to segregated education in the first place will resurface only slightly changed"* (Wright op cit p.4).

There is also a danger that should integrated schools enjoy a financial advantage over other schools there would be a temptation on behalf of schools with a significant minority of the other community to 'change the labels' and become nominally 'integrated', but without any change in ethos. DENI requires only 10% enrolment, from whichever is the minority community, for a school to 'transform' to integrated status, with an expectation that this figure will increase to 70:30 over ten years; still short of the NICIE recommendations.

Paradoxically, Wright argues that integrated education is most likely to flourish if it is not promoted in opposition to the school systems of the two communities (Ibid p.14). Either way, segregated schooling is likely to continue to dominate educational provision for some time to come and other educationalists have therefore proposed an alternative, which is to foster better community relations through cross-curricular developments within denominational schools.

Education for mutual understanding
Since 1983 various activities, formerly promoted by individual teachers and schools to encourage better community relations, have come under the catch-all title of Education for Mutual Understanding. This was given statutory recognition in 1989, under the auspices of the Government's Education Reform (NI) Order, by the introduction of two complementary, cross-curricular themes of Education for Mutual Understanding (EMU) and Cultural Heritage (CH), which formally came into statute in September 1992. Norman Richardson (1997) defines them *"as being fundamentally about learning to live with differences in a spirit of acceptance, fairness and mutual respect"*, which is elaborated by four shared objectives (the

similarity to citizenship education in England and Wales is quite apparent and this is no coincidence):

- Fostering respect for self and others and building relationships, which gives pupils the opportunity 'to develop knowledge and understanding of themselves and how to handle and react appropriately to a range of personal and social situations.'
- Understanding and dealing creatively with conflict, which allows pupils 'to develop knowledge and understanding of conflict in a variety of contexts and how to respond to it positively and creatively.'
- Awareness of interdependence, encouraging pupils 'to develop a knowledge, appreciation and understanding of interdependence, continuity and change in the social and cultural process as it relates to individuals, families, local communities and the wider world.
- Understanding cultural diversity, which develops 'an informed awareness of the similarities and differences between the cultural traditions which influence people who live in Northern Ireland, and the international and trans-national influences on contemporary culture.'

Obviously in developing these cross-curricular themes the content of certain subjects is more relevant than others. The teaching of history, politics and religious studies in particular have often played a central role in perpetuating sectarian division, through omissions and contradictory interpretations. What is required, as McMaster has pointed out, is the application of a 'healthy critical awareness' to the issues raised in these subjects. They need to address the biased presentation of the 'truth' presented by the opposing traditions and allow young people the *"space and freedom to explore political alternatives or options"*. This is particularly true in the case of history, *"which is open to being read from a specific religious or political ideological perspective"* (op cit pp.12-13). While EMU is acknowledged as having played an important role in this regard, crucially by introducing a new vocabulary about respect and tolerance, nevertheless, an evaluation by Smith et. al. (1996) criticised schools for adopting a 'minimalist' approach to EMU, which they attributed to:

- The perception that because the government had imposed it there was a hidden political agenda.
- The lack of 'coherence' and 'progression' associated with the cross-curricular model, which made it disparate and fragmented.
- The lack of a firm basis, which they suggested might be provided by the promotion of civics, human rights and education for democratic participation as a framework.
- The reticence of teachers about addressing issues of violence and sectarianism.
- A lack of appropriate investment in the training and professional development of teachers to support EMU (Smith, A op cit p.6).

To give DENI its due, improved teacher training and the development of a more rigorous framework for EMU has been addressed in a consultation document on the strategic plan for education between 2000 and 2006. Specifically, the introduction of Personal Development and Democratic Education that promotes respect for human rights and democracy. Unfortunately, the obstacles to EMU are not found solely within schools, but reflect the divisions of Northern Irish society. The negative perceptions of teachers, regarding a hidden political agenda, are a prime example and will need to be addressed both within and without the educational system. Even the lack of a coherent framework and adequate teacher training cannot be dealt with entirely within the remit of DENI.

Beside the need for government funds being made available, a common curriculum needs the support of both communities, specifically the teachers who must deliver it.

O'Connor points out that many teachers feel it is almost impossible to create empathy with the 'others' in mono-cultural surroundings (2001).   DENI has attempted to address this issue with the introduction in 1987 of a voluntary inter-school, cross-community contact scheme, which offers financial support to contact programmes between controlled (Protestant) and maintained (Catholic) schools.   While this scheme now covers 54% of Northern Ireland's schools, it is a sad fact that such co-operation often flies in the face of the society's bitter divisions.   In the week following the first disturbances at Holy Cross, the Principal spoke of the efforts she and the head of Wheatfield Primary, a state (Protestant) school across the road, had made to foster mutual civility between their pupils. The latter, however, inextricably linked to its own community, has understandably kept a low profile during the disturbances (O'Connor op cit 2002).

Concluding observations
The role of education in resolving conflict and building sustainable peace in Northern Ireland appears to be caught in a vicious circle. If schools were truly integrated they would be one less institutionalised barrier between the two communities and as such would contribute to improved community relations in the future. True integration can be achieved, however, only with the voluntary support of parents and teachers. Any pressure to conform will be met by resistance and only fuel the existing divisions and distrust of authority. The answer, therefore, appears to lie in fostering education for mutual understanding as a way of reducing tensions between the two communities as a prerequisite for progress toward the goal of shared institutions. The difficulty here of course is trying to foster empathy for the other community in a 'mono-cultural' environment. This can be overcome to an extent by encouraging inter-school, cross-community schemes, but like integrated education it must be voluntary - not forced, otherwise the principle behind it is undermined.

In a paper presented to the American Education Research Association, Alan Smith observed that a classroom teacher in an environment of endemic conflict will have difficulty nurturing tolerance and respect for difference when these basic qualities are absent from society as a whole. Nevertheless, he observed that in Northern Ireland *"there is an expectation that teachers will increasingly find themselves dealing with issues which are socially relevant, related to the conflict and at times, controversial"*, and, in this respect, schools in Northern Ireland are *"part of a more global movement, which looks to education to take account of cultural diversity and conflict within societies"*.

In Britain, he noted, this has been reflected in the debates surrounding multicultural education, anti-racist education and demands from ethnic minorities for separate schools (Smith, A. 1999, p10). The point is that it is fundamentally ineffectual and impractical to place responsibility for escaping the 'circle of hate' on schools and teachers alone. What is required is broader political framework in which education can play its part.

In the case of Northern Ireland this framework has hopefully been provided by the Good Friday Agreement, which represents an attempt to establish new democratic structures to replace the culture of violence that has existed in Northern Ireland over the past thirty years. These structures will only be successful, however, if they contribute to a fair and just society, based upon respect for human rights and diversity.

The implication, therefore, is that there is a need to promote values that support pluralism, human rights and democracy and that education has a vital role to play in this regard. In response to the suggestion that education cannot change society unless the whole structure of society changes and that attempts to initiate change are at best futile and at worst counter-productive, Birgit Brock-Utne replies *"that educational structures are built up of people and that changes must be striven for simultaneously at all levels"*.

She believes that *"personal changes achieve political significance'* and that *'political changes have personal consequences"* (1988, p.96).

Chapter six

A further shore - conclusion

History says, don't hope
On this side of the grave.
But then, once in a lifetime
The longed for tidal wave,
Of justice can rise up,
And hope and history rhyme.

So hope for a great sea-change
On the far side of revenge.
Believe that a further shore
Is reachable from here.
Believe in miracles
And cures and healing wells.

Seamus Heaney, *The Cure at Troy* (Extract)

Summary
The preamble to the UNESCO constitution, quoted at the beginning of the book, states that "...*since wars begin in the minds of men, it is in the minds of men that the defences of peace must be constructed*". In the decade following this declaration, however, Kenneth Waltz challenged its fundamental premise. Essentially he cited three major problems: the problem of pace, the problem of actually instituting change and the problem of dealing with two or more societies at once. In the context of the Cold War these problems were highly significant, but in its aftermath it has been argued that they are by no means insurmountable. Four observations now appear key to discerning the role that

education can play in conflict resolution and in efforts to build sustainable peace:

The nature of conflict and its resolution are multi-faceted
The most significant change since the end of the Cold War has been the increasing incidence of intra-state as opposed to inter-state conflicts.   This new focus has led to a more profound consideration of conflict within states and the fundamental recognition that its causes are a complex mix of four basic components: structural, political, economic and cultural/perceptual. If education is to contribute, therefore, it must do so as part of an overall framework of measures. The role of education in helping to build a sustainable peace in Northern Ireland is a prime example. If it is to make a significant contribution, schools need to be integrated, but encouraging future parents to opt voluntarily for this arrangement in large numbers requires the success of Education for Mutual Understanding (EMU), which is unlikely to happen in its present mono-cultural surroundings. The key appears to be the *Cross Community Contacts Scheme* (CCCS), but this is dependent upon prevailing conditions. The answer is that education must be part of a broader framework of conflict resolution initiatives, which are bound within a political agreement between the two communities. At least in Northern Ireland there is such an agreement, however imperfect.

Perhaps the best way of envisioning this multi-faceted approach is as suggested by Liechty and Clegg, who observe that *"situations of endemic conflict, as in Northern Ireland, are best thought of as analogous to ecosystems. In studying an ecosystem the pursuit of the fundamental would be nonsense, because the focus is on relationships between parts in the context of the whole system"* (op cit p.61). Nevertheless, this particular type of ecosystem, because it is entirely man-made, does have a common thread running through it: namely the role of identity, which leads us to the second observation.

Negative identity

Identity, a sense of self and a sense of relationship to the world and to others, is basic to humanity, but it can be constructed either positively or negatively. Identity is as much about what a person is, as it is about what he or she is not. If this negative aspect of identity rises to such a pitch that the 'other' is seen as a threat to your own identity then it will lead to conflict and violence. The power of negative identity lies in the very fact that it has its roots in a genuine human need and cannot therefore be destroyed, but instead must be transformed in order to support and sustain co-operation and peace. This is where education can play its part, by helping to transform negative constructions of identity into more positive ones. Liechty and Clegg are persuaded that this is crucial, because although *"the relationship between action and thought, the external and the internal, between the public manifestation and inner logic, is not easily determined ... outward changes are most likely to endure when they are accompanied by inward transformation"* (op cit p.338). It has been demonstrated throughout this book, however, that not all 'education' will lead us out of the 'circle of hate', and we must therefore consider a third observation.

Education can be both good and bad

At an extreme, those who seek power or who wish to secure their position in power often nurture the negative power of resistance identities: the rise and ascendancy of the Nazis in Germany being an obvious example. In educational terms this manifests itself in indoctrination, the antithesis of any positive notion of education. At a less extreme pitch, the promotion of legitimising identities is far more common. Whether in a realist or liberal guise, the goal is to habituate people to the current social, economic and political system and therefore suppress conflict. Liberalism may promote change, but this is purely for individual and national gain within the present system. The power of this approach is that it purports to present the world as it unalterably is and therefore condemns any attempt to change the underlying system as futile. Critical theorists, however, dispute this and attempt to identify and support processes that can potentially lead to systemic change.

The role of education in building sustainable peace is concerned with the transformation of perceptions and attitudes, consequently Critical Theory is important because it allows us to envision choices beyond those legitimised by the dominant group. Of specific help is Habermas's notion of dialogue, which widens choice by encouraging reflection and positive communication, enabling people to escape the narrow confines of the self by making sense of their own experiences and those of other people; likewise, Linklater's belief in our capacity to expand the moral boundaries of our notions of community; and finally, in a purely educational context, Paulo Friere's critique of the 'banking' concept of education and his conviction that if people are encouraged to transform themselves they will begin to transform society. This conviction is fundamental and is the final observation.

People's attitudes can change for the better
While it is important to underline the fact that *"there are no magical ways of overcoming national divisions through educational systems"* (Wright 1991, p.14), it is nevertheless reasonable to believe that a change in people's attitudes is possible. In the words of Liechty and Clegg, *"an historical account shows that sectarianism, while the product of powerful forces, was not inevitable. It resulted from concrete choices people made, and which they might have made differently. We cannot undo the past, but we can make different choices now to shape a different future"* (op cit p.100). This belief was most graphically supported by the positive aspects of human behaviour exhibited during and after the events of 11 September 2001. Education must nurture these compassionate and selfless aspects of human behaviour.

Recommendations for action: 'cures and healing wells'
Whichever metaphor is used, escaping the 'circle of hate' or reaching a 'further shore', the message is clear: in addressing conflict we need to be someplace other than where we are now. Central to this vision is the necessity for a transformation of our present world-view from one primarily focused on conflict to one focused primarily on cooperation. It is not suggested that by envisioning utopia we will achieve it; society is too uneasy a compromise between individuals with conflicting ambitions for this to be the case. Nevertheless, while humans can be self-interested and anti-social, they also have some instincts which foster the greater good. In designing an education system we should therefore aim to discourage the former and encourage the latter. The promotion of three aptitudes of mind appear critical to this endeavour and should therefore underpin any educational programme aimed at building sustainable peace: reflection, vision and creativity.

- Reflection is the first aptitude, because before people can move to a 'further shore' they need to know where they are now. Reflection helps and encourages people to understand their environment, themselves and others, which in turn helps them to cope with uncertainty. Donald Schon (1983), who has done a great deal of work on the role of reflection, describes it as a capacity within people *"to cope with and shape change and uncertainty by interpreting and responding to the particularities of the circumstances they find"*. Self-understanding is fundamental, for without it there is little hope of mutual understanding. In Northern Ireland, Liechty and Clegg have argued that everyone is implicated in sectarianism to one degree or another. It is crucial, therefore, that individuals take active responsibility for their own complicity, *"working at self-awareness, self-critique, radical honesty, and developing ongoing reflective methodologies that will expose complicity"* (op cit p.343).

- The second aptitude is vision, because having established where we are, we need to know where we are going. Vision supplies the motivation for change and is best explained in the words of Liechty and Clegg:

"It is a fairly simple psychological truth that people will not change if they do not have a vision of what it is that they are changing to, moving toward, becoming. In the absence of such a vision, they will, to a remarkable extent, prefer the devil they know to the devil they don't. They may even prefer the devil they know and dislike to the rumour of some great thing if they cannot see how they could possibly get there. No vision, no change – even though people may rail against their present situation. When captivated by a vision, on the other hand, the changes people are capable of are amazing" (op cit p.337).

Sentiments mirrored by Lederach's concept of generational change (see Lederach's Nested Paradigm in Chapter 2).

- The final element is creativity, which allows us to envisage ways of moving from our present position to somewhere new. Anna Craft describes creativity as flux, change, development and growth. More importantly she believes that it describes an approach to life that begins with 'perhaps if'… or 'what if'… and she characterises this 'questioning core of creativity' as 'possibility thinking' (1997 p.9). This means two things: first, the ability to use your imagination to find solutions to problems and second the ability to ask questions. Craft quotes Professor Philip Gammage, who suggests that education should not be about 'answering the question', but rather about 'questioning the answer' (Ibid p.7). The ability to question authority and dogmatism is essential if we are to break away from the 'circle of hate'. In the conclusion to his book *Hitler's Children*, Guido Knopp quotes Gregor

Dorfmeister, a member of the Hitlerjunge, who was sixteen at the end of the war. Dorfmeister recounts: *"I often come up against the question of our motivation, and a 'cool' teenager of today naturally asks, why were you so stupid as to go along with it? I can only reply: thank God you are able to ask that question today. We couldn't have asked it then"* (op cit p.283). It is vital that we are not be imprisoned by stereotypical visions of what we perceive reality to be, nor succumb to the fatalistic view that the world is as it is, and cannot be otherwise. Bill Williamson uses the analogy of successful companies, which develop new ways of solving problems and realise that investment in creative minds is central to their survival (op cit p.107). In the same way communities that strengthen their capacity to think creatively are the most likely to envisage an alternative to the circle of hate.

The aim of education, therefore, should be to unite these three elements in order to enable individuals and communities to escape the circle of hate. This, I believe, can be achieved through Futures Education, specifically the concept of the Transformation Cycle (Beare and Slaughter, 1993, pp.135-8). In many ways it is a positive mirror of the 'circle of hate', allowing us to envisage the means by which we can escape the cycle of violent conflict (see below). Futurists, as Wendell Bell explains, encourage reflection, vision and creativity by challenging people *"to examine critically their current routines of behaviour, to consider alternatives, to search for currently unrecognised possibilities, to analyse their goals and values, to become more conscious of the future and the control they may have over it, and to care about the freedom and well-being of future generations"* (Ibid p.23).

New States
of Being

Breakdown of Meaning

Generational Vision
(20+ years)

Reconceptualisations

Disputes and Negotiation

Failed
suggestions

Rejected suggestions

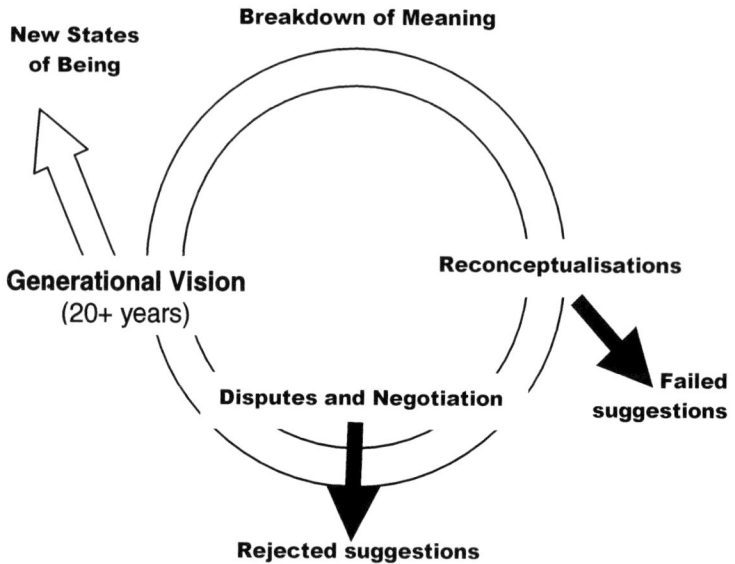

6.1 Transformation Cycle or T- Cycle (adapted by the author)

The Transformation or 'T-Cycle' begins from the premise
that we are going through a period characterised by
uncertainty and anxiety generated by unemployment, stress,
racism, crime, poverty and apparent meaninglessness,
equally it could apply to a pre-conflict or post-conflict
environment. Whatever the case, there is a recognition that
unless individuals and society confront this 'breakdown of
meaning' the result will be depression, anger and violence,
which are characteristic of 'resistance identities'. By
bringing the breakdown to full consciousness we are able to
search our cultural environment for anything that might be
useful in resolving our problems and ultimately to envisage
new choices and possibilities, in other words, it is a process
of **reflection** leading to new **visions** of the future. This then
leads us into the second **creative** stage where these visions
are explored, thereby helping us to reconceptualise our
situation and address the breakdown. At this point many
proposals will fail because they are inappropriate or
impractical. Nevertheless in considering possible solutions

we set up possibilities that invite individual and societal responses and this moves us onto the third stage. This phase is a winnowing process of dispute and negotiation. Disputes occur because the new impacts on the old and someone's interests are always bound up in the way things are. In other words, a clash occurs between legitimising and project identities, which results in the final stage, that of 'selective legitimation'. This reflects the outcome of the dispute, and refers to the way some innovations and proposals are accepted while others are discarded. The question, of course, and the one that I have addressed throughout this book, is whether this 'selective legitimation' leads to another breakdown and further violent conflict, or a 'new state of being' beyond the 'circle of hate'.

In his inaugural lecture, to the Chair of International Education at Birmingham University (May 2002), Clive Harber observed that in order to ensure positive transformations, we must consider the ideological context. He used the salient example of a terrorist training camp, which could well produce reflective, visionary and creative individuals, but to what end? I agree; reflection, vision and creativity are no guarantee of sustainable peace unless given a positive ideological context. If we are to achieve sustainable peace, education must encourage the positive side of human nature through the promotion of a 'culture of peace' and the principles of democracy. The difficulty is that there is no guarantee that people will choose peace and democracy, and, in an era of cultural relativity, any attempt to manipulate peoples' choice runs the risk of accusations of cultural arrogance and even indoctrination. The answer therefore rests upon choice.

Education is about choice. At a practical level passing exams offers choices about future study and employment, but more importantly education offers choices about how to behave, build relationships and relate to fellow human beings. As pointed out in Chapter 5, sectarianism is not inevitable; it is about concrete choices that have been made in the past. The crucial point is that different choices can be made in the future. The role of education is to give people as wide a range of choice as possible, not reinforce existing patterns of behaviour and thought. By fostering reflection, vision and creativity, education expands the horizons of individuals and, by extension, communities. As Miss Jean Brodie declares in Muriel Spark's novel, education is about leading out what is already there within children, not putting something in. Compassion and the capacity for peaceful relations are as much a part of human nature as aggression and the capacity for violent conflict, but at present we tend to emphasise the latter at the expense of the former. If we are to escape the 'circle of hate' education must right the balance by offering the choice of peace.

Bibliography

Interviews

Clive Harber, Professor of International Education, Birmingham University - Interviewed on 11 July 2002 at the School of Education, Birmingham University. This interview followed Professor Harber's inaugural lecture to the Chair of International Education on 16 May 2002, which was also of immense assistance.

Academic Papers

Aguilar, P. & Retamol, G. *Rapid Educational Responses in Complex Emergencies,* (International Bureau for Education, Switzerland 1998)

Bellamy, C. *Global Security MSc Course Handbook* (Cranfield University, academic year 2001-2002)

Blair, S. *Weaving the Strands of the Rope* (MSc Global Security dissertation for the academic year 2000/2001, Cranfield University)

Larkin, C. *Citizenship Education or Crowd Control,* (Centre for Conflict Resolution, Bradford University, July 2001)

Singer, P.W. 'Pakistan's Madrassahs: Ensuring a System of Education not Jihad' Analysis Paper 14, November 2001, Brookings Institute

Stovel, L. *Confronting Ethnic Chauvinism in a Post-War Environment: NGOs and Peace Education in Bosnia* (Department of Peace Studies, University of Bradford, December 2000)

MA in Education Study Guide, Module E827 (Open University, academic year 1999-2000)

Papers from Conferences

Harris, I. 'Challenges for Peace Educators at the Beginning of the Twenty-First Century' - paper presented at the Annual Meeting of the *Educational Research Association* (Seattle, WA, 10-14th April, 2001)

1

Kerr, D. 'Citizenship Education and the Revised National Curriculum' paper prepared for NFER Annual Conference (6 October 1998)

Smith, A. 'Education and the Peace Process in Northern Ireland' paper presented to the Annual Conference of the American Education Research Association, Montreal, April 1999.

Official Reports and Documents (see also internet sources)

Education in Kosova Report to the British Council, Professor Lynn Davies (School of Education, University of Birmingham 3 August 1999)

The Agreement, document sent to all citizens of Northern Ireland by the Northern Ireland Office prior to the referendum on the Good Friday Agreement, no publication details.

Books and Monographs

Barash, D. P. (2000) *Approaches to Peace,* Oxford: Oxford University Press

Baylis, J. & Smith, S. (ed) (2001) *The Globalisation of World Politics,* Oxford: Oxford University Press

Beare, H. & Slaughter, R. (1993) *Education for the Twenty-First Century,* London: Routledge

Bell, D. (1990) *Acts of Union,* London: MacMillan

Bellamy, C. (1998) *Spiral Through Time: Beyond 'Conflict Intensity',* Strategic and Combat Studies Institute, Occasional Paper, No 35 p.33

Boulding, E. (ed) (1992) *New Agendas for Peace Research,* Boulder, Colorado: Lynne Rienner Publishers Inc.

Briscoe, M. (1963) *Rocket Propulsion,* London: Chatto and Windus Ltd.

Brock-Utne, B. (1988) 'Formal education as a force in shaping cultural norms relating to war and the environment'

2

in *Cultural Norms, War and the Environment,* Westing A.H. (ed) SIPRI, Oxford University Press

Brown. M. E. et al. (ed) (2001) *Nationalism and Ethnic Conflict,* Harvard College and MIT Press

Burchill, S. et al. (2001) *Theories of International Relations,* Hampshire: Palgrave

Castells, M. (2001) *The Power of Identity,* Oxford: Blackwell Ltd.

Cohen, R. & Kennedy, P. (2000) *Global Sociology,* New York: Palgrave

Cox R.W. (1993) 'Gramsci, Hegemony and International Relations: an essay in method' in *Gramsci, Historical Materialism and International Relations,* Gill,S (ed) Press Syndicate of the University of Cambridge

Craft, A. (1997) *Can You Teach Creativity?* Nottingham: Education Now Publishing Co-operative

Curle, A. (1995) *Another way: positive response to contemporary violence,* Oxford: Jon Carpenter

Devetak, R. et al. (2001) *Theories of International Relations,* Hampshire: Palgrave

Downing, T. (ed) (1989) *The Troubles,* London: Maxwell & Co. Publishers

Dunne, T. (2001) 'Liberalism' in *The Globalisation of World Politics,* Baylis, J. and Smith, S. (eds) Oxford University Press

Fraser, G. & Morgan, V. (1999) *In the Frame: Integrated Education in Northern Ireland,* University of Ulster, Coleraine

Freire, P. (1996) *Pedagogy of the Oppressed,* London: Penguin Books Ltd.

Gill, S. (ed) (1993) *Historical Materialism and International Relations,* Press Syndicate of the University of Cambridge, Cambridge

3

Green, A. (1990) *Education and State Formation,* London: Macmillan

Green, A. (1997) *Education, Globalisation and the Nation-State,* London: Macmillan

Haydon, G. (1999) *Values, Virtues and Violence: Education and the Public Understanding of Morality,* London: Blackwell Publishers

Hinde, R.A. (1990) 'Human Aggression: Biological Propensities and Social Force' in *A Reader in Peace Studies,* Smoker, P. et al (ed) Oxford, Pergamon Press

Hobden, S. & Wyn-Jones, R. (2001) 'Marxist Theories of International Relations' in Baylis, J. & Smith, S. (ed) *The Globalisation of World Politics,* Oxford; Oxford University Press

Hutchinson, F. P. (1996) *Educating Beyond Violent Futures,* London: Routledge

Jones, C. & Kennedy-Pipe, C. (ed) (2000) *International Security in a Global Age,* London: Frank Cass Publishers

Knopp, G. (2002) *Hitler's Children,* (English translation) Sutton Publishing Ltd.

Knox, C. & Quirk, P. (2000) *Peace building in Northern Ireland, Israel and South Africa,* London: MacMillan Press

Lederach, J. P. (1999) *Building Peace,* Washington: United States Institute of Peace

Liechty, J. & Clegg, C. (2001) *Moving Beyond Sectarianism,* Dublin: The Colomba Press

Linklater, A. et al. (2001) *Theories of International Relations,* Hampshire: Palgrave

Linklater, A. (1998) *The Transformation of Political Community: Ethical Foundations of the Post-Westphalian Era,* Cambridge

Low-Beer, A. (2001) 'Politics, school textbooks and cultural identity: the struggle in Bosnia and Hercegovina.' in *Textbook Research* No.2

4

McMaster, J. (1993) *Young People as the Guardians of Sectarian Tradition,* Booklet Number 2, NI: Youth Link

Meighan, R. (1995) *The Freethinkers' Guide to the Educational Universe,* Nottingham: Educational Heretics Press

O'Connor, F. (2001) *A Shared Childhood – The story of integrated schools in Northern Ireland,* Belfast: Blackstaff Press in association with the Integrated Education Fund

Pring, R. (1984) *Personal and Social Education in the Curriculum,* London: Hodder & Stoughton

Rupesinghe, K. (1992) 'The Disappearing Boundaries Between Internal and External Conflicts, in *New Agendas for Peace Research*, Boulder, Colarado: Lynne Rienner Publishers Inc,

Reardon, B. (1985) *Sexism and the War System,* New York: Teachers College Press

Robertson, D. (1985) *Dictionary of Politics,* Harmondsworth: Penguin Books Ltd.

Rogers, A. (1986) *Teaching Adults,* Buckingham: Open University Press

SIPRI Yearbook 2000, Oxford: Oxford University Press

Schon, D. (1983) *The Reflective Practitioner: How Professionals Think in Action,* London; Basic Books

Smith, H. (1986) *The Russians,* London: Times Books

Smith, S. et al. (ed) (1996) *International theory: positivism and beyond,* Cambridge: Press Syndicate of the University of Cambridge

Smoker, P. et al. (ed) (1990) *A Reader in Peace Studies,* Oxford: Pergamon Press

Spark, M. (1965) *The Prime of Miss Jean Brodie,* London: Penguin Books

Waltz, K. N. (2001) *Man the State and War,* New York: Columbia University Press

Westing, A.H. (ed) (1988) *Cultural Norms, War and the Environment,* Oxford: SIPRI, Oxford University Press

Williamson, B. (2001) *Lifeworlds and Learning,* Leicester: National Institute of Adult Education

Wright, F. (1991) *Integrated Education,* Northern Ireland: Corrymeela Press

Articles from Journals

Berlowitz, M. 'Urban educational reform: Focusing on peace education' in *Education and Urban Society,* (27(1), 1994)

Bloom, W. 'Personal Identity, National Identity and International Relations' in *Cambridge Studies in International Relations* 9/1990

Harber, C. 'Schooling as Violence: an explanatory overview' in *Educational Review* (Volume 54, No. 1, 2002)

Lord Robertson 'NATO in the New Millennium and Security in the World' in *Military Technology* 1/2001

Newspaper Articles (see also internet sources)

Angier, N. 'Why we can't help but help each other' *The Guardian* 22 September 2001, Review Section

Castle, S. 'How the Extremists have thrown another rock in the pool' in *The Independent* 23 April 2002

Cornwell, R. 'So this is history' in *The Independent* 7 Jan 2002

Dawkins, R. 'Our big brains can overcome our selfish genes' *The Independent* 12 February 2002

Hartley-Brewer, E. 'It's good to talk, better to listen' *The Independent* 21 February 2002

McCarthy, M. 'Ulster's sectarianism worsens in peaceful times' *The Independent* 4 January 2002

Macintyre, D. 'It takes generations to change bigotry' *The Independent* 9 September 2001

McKittrick, D. 'Cowering schoolgirls given lesson in sectarian brutality' *The Independent* 11 January 2002

6

McKittrick, D. 'In this divided city, segregation has become a way of life over centuries' *The Independent* 4 January 2002

O'Connor, F. 'Repeat after me: A is for Apartheid' *The Independent* 9 September 2001

Orr, D. 'Voices of moderation and reason are being drowned out by the demagogues' *The Independent* 8 May 2002

Smithers, R 'Police to be based in schools blighted by truancy' *The Guardian* 30 April 2002

Author not named 'How can we tackle Islamic Extremism?' *Sunday Times* 7 October 2001

Author not named 'How sick is Europe' *The Economist* 11–17th May 2002

Internet Sources

Richardson, N. L. 'Education for Mutual Understanding and Cultural Heritage' *CAIN Web Service* 1997
http://cain.ulst.ac.uk/emu/emuback.htm p.2

Brookings Institute
http://www.brook.edu/dybdocroot/views/papers/singer/20020103.htm

CAIN Web Service
http://cain.ulst.ac.uk/emu/emuback.htm

Department for Education of Northern Ireland, *Literature Review: Integrated Education in Northern Ireland* (Research Briefing 3/99
http://www.deni.gov.uk/facts_figures/research/rb1999_3.htm)

DfEE website
http://www.nc.uk.net/about/about_citizenship.html

NICIE Website *Planned Integrated Education*
http://www.nicie.org/files/rightside.htm

Observer internet edition
http://www.observer.co.uk/nireland/story/0,11008,582085,00.html

UNESCO website
http://www.unesco.org/iycp/uk/uk_cp.htm

APPENDIX 1

Citizenship Education KEY STAGE 3

Knowledge, skills and understanding

Teaching should ensure that **knowledge and understanding about becoming informed citizens** are acquired and applied when **developing skills of enquiry and communication, and participation and responsible action**.

Knowledge and understanding about becoming informed citizens

1. Pupils should be taught about:

a. the legal and human rights and responsibilities underpinning society, basic aspects of the criminal justice system, and how both relate to young people
b. the diversity of national, regional, religious and ethnic identities in the United Kingdom and the need for mutual respect and understanding
c. central and local government, the public services they offer and how they are financed, and the opportunities to contribute
d. the key characteristics of parliamentary and other forms of government
e. the electoral system and the importance of voting
f. the work of community-based, national and international voluntary groups
g. the importance of resolving conflict fairly
h. the significance of the media in society
i. the world as a global community, and the political, economic, environmental and social implications of this, and the role of the European Union, the Commonwealth and the United Nations.

Developing skills of enquiry and communication

2. Pupils should be taught to:
a. think about topical political, spiritual, moral, social and cultural issues, problems and events by analysing information and its sources, including ICT-based sources

b. justify orally and in writing a personal opinion about such issues, problems or events

c. contribute to group and exploratory class discussions, and take part in debates.

Developing skills of participation and responsible action

3. Pupils should be taught to:

a. use their imagination to consider other people's experiences and be able to think about, express and explain views that are not their own

b. negotiate, decide and take part responsibly in both school and community-based activities

c. reflect on the process of participating

APPENDIX 2

Citizenship Education KEY STAGE 4

Knowledge, skills and understanding

Teaching should ensure that **knowledge and understanding about becoming informed citizens** are acquired and applied when **developing skills of enquiry and communication**, and **participation and responsible action**.

Knowledge and understanding about becoming informed citizens

1. Pupils should be taught about:

a. the legal and human rights and responsibilities underpinning society and how they relate to citizens, including the role and operation of the criminal and civil justice systems

b. the origins and implications of the diverse national, regional, religious and ethnic identities in the United Kingdom and the need for mutual respect and understanding

c. the work of parliament, the government and the courts in making and shaping the law

d. the importance of playing an active part in democratic and electoral processes

e. how the economy functions, including the role of business and financial services

f. the opportunities for individuals and voluntary groups to bring about social change locally, nationally, in Europe and internationally

g. the importance of a free press, and the media's role in society, including the internet, in providing information and affecting opinion

h. the rights and responsibilities of consumers, employers and employees

i. the United Kingdom's relations in Europe, including the European Union, and relations with the Commonwealth and the United Nations

j. the wider issues and challenges of global interdependence and responsibility, including sustainable development and Local Agenda 21.

Developing skills of enquiry and communication

2. Pupils should be taught to:

a. research a topical political, spiritual, moral, social or cultural issue, problem or event by analysing information from different sources, including ICT-based sources, showing an awareness of the use and abuse of statistics

b. express, justify and defend orally and in writing a personal opinion about such issues, problems or events

c. contribute to group and exploratory class discussions, and take part in formal debates.

Developing skills of participation and responsible action

3. Pupils should be taught to:

a. use their imagination to consider other people's experiences and be able to think about, express, explain and critically evaluate views that are not their own

b. negotiate, decide and take part responsibly in school and community-based activities

c. reflect on the process of participating.

APPENDIX 3

Culture of Peace

As defined by the United Nations, the **Culture of Peace is a set of values, attitudes, modes of behaviour and ways of life that reject violence and prevent conflicts by tackling their root causes to solve problems through dialogue and negotiation among individuals, groups and nations** (UN Resolutions A/RES/52/13: Culture of Peace and A/RES/53/243, Declaration and Programme of Action on a Culture of Peace). For peace and non-violence to prevail, we need to:

foster a culture of peace through education

by revising the educational curricula to promote qualitative values, attitudes and behaviours of a culture of peace, including peaceful conflict-resolution, dialogue, consensus-building and active non-violence. Such an educational approach should be geared also to:

promote sustainable economic and social development

by reducing economic and social inequalities, by eradicating poverty and by assuring sustainable food security, social justice, durable solutions to debt problems, empowerment of women, special measures for groups with special needs, environmental sustainability...

promote respect for all human rights

human rights and a culture of peace are complementary: whenever war and violence dominate, there is no possibility to ensure human rights; at the same time, without human rights, in all their dimensions, there can be no culture of peace...

ensure equality between women and men

through full participation of women in economic, social and political decision-making, elimination of all forms of discrimination and violence against women, support and assistance to women in need...

foster democratic participation

indispensable foundations for the achievement and maintenance of peace and security are democratic principles, practices and participation in all sectors of society, a transparent and accountable governance and administration, the combat against terrorism, organized crime, corruption, illicit drugs and money laundering...

advance understanding, tolerance and solidarity

to abolish war and violent conflicts we need to transcend and overcome enemy images with understanding, tolerance and solidarity among all peoples and cultures. Learning from our differences, through dialogue and the exchange of information, is an enriching process...

support participatory communication and the free flow of information and knowledge

freedom of information and communication and the sharing of information and knowledge are indispensable for a culture of peace. However, measures need to be taken to address the issue of violence in the media, including new information and communication technologies...

promote international peace and security

the gains in human security and disarmament in recent years, including nuclear weapons treaties and the treaty banning land mines, should encourage us to increase our efforts in negotiation of peaceful settlements, elimination of production and traffic of arms and weapons, humanitarian solutions in conflict situations, post-conflict initiatives...